The Young Scholar's Workbook

Book I Vol. I

By

Brenda Diann Johnson

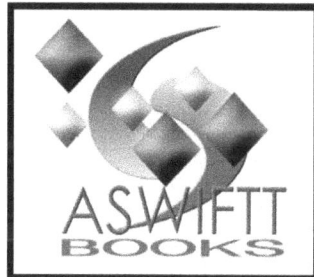

ASWIFTT ENTERPRISES, LLC
Duncanville, Texas 75138

Brenda Diann Johnson
E-mail: brendadiannjohnson@yahoo.com

ASWIFTT ENTERPRISES, LLC
Imprint: ASWIFTT BOOKS
P.O. Box 380669
Duncanville, Texas 75138-0669

ISBN: 978-0-9847015-0-6

Printed in the United States of America

All lessons in this workbook mirror The Young Scholar's Book Club educational curriculum for Pre-K to 4th grade. Some lessons are aligned with the Texas Essentials Knowledge & Skills (TEKS) curriculum.

All Workbook clipart provided by Jupiter Images
Authentic drawings and editing provided by Brenda Diann Johnson
Assistant editing provided by Kamille Padgitt

Fundraiser

The Young Scholar's Workbook: Book I Vol. I is a fundraiser workbook for **The Young Scholar's Book Club**. 50% of all proceeds are donated to TYSBC to keep the online education program for tutoring and mentoring free to students. The workbook has assignments for Pre-K to 4th grade.

The Young Scholar's Book Club is a free online educational program for Pre-K to 4th grade. The program offers reading enrichment, tutoring assignments, vocabulary-building skills, analytical and critical thinking skills and a whole lot more.

TYS Book Club provides encouragement and support. Students are provided with a monthly reading schedule, a book assignment, weekly tutoring worksheets in all core subjects, feedback, awards for doing well, workshops and more. The program provides its services via the internet, regular mail and summer workshops.

The program runs from August to May. During June and July, **The Young Scholar's Book Club** offers workshops, seminars and other activities for its members. The program can be accessed on our website at **www.tysbookclub.com**

For more information on **The Young Scholar's Book Club** write:
P.O. Box 380669
Duncanville, Texas 75138

Dedications

I dedicate **The Young Scholar's Workbook: Book I Vol. I** to Diamond and Kamille. They are my inspiration to educate children. I strive to be the best mother and teacher to my girls because mother and teacher go hand in hand.

Table of Contents

Section I: Pre-K to Kindergarten

Foreword

"Make a Difference……Teach?"

When I read the motto, "Make a Difference……Teach?" I immediately see a question proposed by the motto. When I look at the motto more closely, I notice that it is two-fold. It makes a bold statement to make a difference and it proposes a question to the reader.

First, the motto is meant to encourage and boldly challenge the reader to make a difference in the world. Second, the motto proposes the question, Teach? Is teaching the answer to making a difference in the world?

I believe the statement and question proposed in the motto is thought provoking. In fact, in order to make a difference in the world, we must continue to educate. We specifically need to educate those who have influence and those who will have influence on how our nation operates.

Those who have influence on our nation today are our federal, state, and city leaders. These leaders run our nation. They have been trained and educated by teachers in the past to help validate their job credentials.

We rely on our leaders to do a good job and to be knowledgeable in making the right decisions for the country as a whole.

It is in the best interest of the nation for our leaders to continue educating themselves throughout their careers. Many enroll in continuing education courses to gain new knowledge and to stay up to date on current issues. Some leaders rely on advisors to help them stay abreast on current issues and new information. In our formal educational institutions, teachers will always play a role in educating those who lead our nation. Informal education is also a benefit. Leaders must do their own research and personal study to make educated decisions when it comes to our nation.

Teachers help shape our nation by educating and preparing our children for the future. Our children are educated in our public and private school systems. They will also be educated in our formal educational institutions beyond high school.

In order for our children to make a difference in our nation, they need to be educated and prepared by individuals, who will boldly accept the challenge.

Teachers are responsible for staying up to date in subjects like Science and Technology, History, Mathematics, Social Sciences, Language Arts, and other subjects as well. Knowledge imparted to children through good teachers will have a positive and powerful impact on our nation in the future.

Teachers not only play a role in formally educating our children, but they also educate our children informally. Teachers have a lot to do with shaping our children's attitudes and beliefs about our nation and the society we live in. From Pre-K through college, attitudes and beliefs are being shaped.

Teachers educate and train children about our nation's past mistakes, present, and mistakes that will be made if the same actions are repeated. Teachers help children analyze and think through problems. They also help encourage children to come up with solutions to problems. Teachers are valuable to our nation. It is because of teachers that our children will know how to fully play out their future roles in society.

Brenda Diann Johnson

ix

How To Use This Workbook

1. The Young Scholar's Workbook: Book I Vol. I is divided into 2 sections: Pre-K to Kindergarten & 1st to 4th grade. All lessons were written from TYS Book Club curriculum and some lessons are aligned with The Texas Essentials Knowledge & Skills (TEKS) curriculum.
2. Read the directions for each lesson.
3. Follow the directions exactly as they appear in this workbook for each lesson.
4. Purchase or check out the books and materials needed from your local store, bookstore or library.
5. Ask parents or guardians for help if you don't understand a lesson.
6. Pre-K and Kindergarten parents, guardians, or educators must either read or assist with the books in the reading section of this workbook. Parents, guardians, or educators must also assist with the questions in the reading section and other lessons.
7. You can e-mail the curriculum department with any questions concerning the material in this workbook at: **tysbookclub@yahoo.com**
8. Please allow 7 business days for a response to your e-mail.

9. Students please attempt to do all lessons on your own before looking at the answer key.

Please write or e-mail *The Young Scholar's Book Club* with any suggestions, comments or feedback on material you would like to see in our next workbook.

10. Parents, guardians and educators can re-produce copies of lessons in this workbook for educational purposes only and not commercial. Any unauthorized use of the material in this workbook is illegal and subject to legal actions.

Write to or e-mail: **The Young Scholar's Book Club**
P.O. Box 380669
Duncanville, Texas 75138-0669
E-Mail: **tysbookclub@yahoo.com**

Section I: Pre-K to Kindergarten

Language Arts

Name_____ Date_____

Practice writing the Capital Letter A on the line. The first one is
an example. *{TYS LA Pre-K to K, Pre-K LA III.C.1, III.C.2, III.C.3, IV.B.2, K
110.2(b)(5)(e), K 110.2(b)(14)(a)(b), K 110.2(b)(7)(a), K 110.2(b)(7)(c)}*

A <u>AAAAAAAAAAAAAAAA</u>

A_____

A_____

What sound does the letter /**Aa**/ make? Say it aloud.

Practice writing the lower case a on the line. The first one is an
example.

<u>aaaaaaaaaaaaaaaaaaaaaaaaa</u>

a_____

a_____

Name_____Date_____

Practice writing the Capital Letter **B** on the line. The first one is an example. *{TYS LA Pre-K to K, Pre-K LA III.C.1, III.C.2, III.C.3, IV.B.2, K 110.2(b)(5)(e), K 110.2(b)(14)(a)(b), K 110.2(b)(7)(a), K 110.2(b)(7)(c)}*

B B B B B B B B B B B B B

B_____

B_____

What sound does the letter /**Bb**/ make? Say it aloud.

Practice writing the lower case **b** on the line. The first one is an example.

b bbbbbbbbbbbbbbbb

b_____

b_____

Name_____Date_____

Practice writing the Capital Letter **C** on the line. The first one is an example. *{TYS LA Pre-K to K, Pre-K LA III.C.1, III.C.2, III.C.3, IV.B.2, K 110.2(b)(5)(e), K 110.2(b)(14)(a)(b), K 110.2(b)(7)(a), K 110.2(b)(7)(c)}*

C <u>CCCCCCCCCCCCCC</u>

C _____

C _____

What sound does the letter /**Cc**/ make? Say it aloud.

Practice writing the lower case **C** on the line. The first one is an example.

C <u>CCCCCCCCCCCCCCCCCCCC</u>

C _____

C _____

Name_____ Date_____

Practice writing the Capital Letter **D** on the line. The first one is an example. *{TYS LA Pre-K to K, Pre-K LA III.C.1, III.C.2, III.C.3, IV.B.2, K 110.2(b)(5)(e), K 110.2(b)(14)(a)(b), K 110.2(b)(7)(a), K 110.2(b)(7)(c)}*

D <u>DDDDDDDDDDDDDD</u>

D _____

D _____

What sound does the letter /**Dd**/ make? Say it aloud.

Practice writing the lower case **d** on the line. The first one is an example.

d <u>dddddddddddddddddd</u>

d _____

d _____

Name_____Date_____

Practice writing the Capital Letter **E** on the line. The first one is an example. *{TYS LA Pre-K to K, Pre-K LA III.C.1, III.C.2, III.C.3, IV.B.2, K 110.2(b)(5)(e), K 110.2(b)(14)(a)(b), K 110.2(b)(7)(a), K 110.2(b)(7)(c)}*

E <u>EEEEEEEEEEEEEEEEEE</u>

E _____

E _____

What sound does the letter /**Ee**/ make? Say it aloud.

Practice writing the lower case **e** on the line. The first one is an example.

e <u>eeeeeeeeeeeeeeeeeeeee</u>

e _____

e _____

Name_____ Date_____

Practice writing the Capital Letter **F** on the line. The first one is an example. *{TYS LA Pre-K to K, Pre-K LA III.C.1, III.C.2, III.C.3, IV.B.2, K 110.2(b)(5)(e), K 110.2(b)(14)(a)(b), K 110.2(b)(7)(a), K 110.2(b)(7)(c)}*

F F F F F F F F F F F F F

F _____

F _____

What sound does the letter /**Ff**/ make? Say it aloud.

Practice writing the lower case **f** on the line. The first one is an example.

f f f f f f f f f f f f f f f f f f f f f

f _____

f _____

Name_____Date_____

Practice writing the Capital Letter **G** on the line. The first one is an example. *{TYS LA Pre-K to K, Pre-K LA III.C.1, III.C.2, III.C.3, IV.B.2, K 110.2(b)(5)(e), K 110.2(b)(14)(a)(b), K 110.2(b)(7)(a), K 110.2(b)(7)(c)}*

G GGGGGGGGGGGGGG

G _____

G _____

What sound does the letter /**Gg**/ make? Say it aloud.

Practice writing the lower case **g** on the line. The first one is an example.

g ggggggggggggggggggggggg

g _____

g _____

Name_____Date_____

Practice writing the Capital Letter H on the line. The first one is an example. *{TYS LA Pre-K to K, Pre-K LA III.C.1, III.C.2, III.C.3, IV.B.2, K 110.2(b)(5)(e), K 110.2(b)(14)(a)(b), K 110.2(b)(7)(a), K 110.2(b)(7)(c)}*

H HHHHHHHHHHHHHHHH

H _____

H _____

What sound does the letter /**Hh**/ make? Say it aloud.

Practice writing the lower case h on the line. The first one is an example.

h hhhhhhhhhhhhhhhhhh

h _____

h _____

The Young Scholar's Book Club

Name_____ Date_____

Practice writing the Capital Letter I on the line. The first one is an example. *{TYS LA Pre-K to K, Pre-K LA III.C.1, III.C.2, III.C.3, IV.B.2, K 110.2(b)(5)(e), K 110.2(b)(14)(a)(b), K 110.2(b)(7)(a), K 110.2(b)(7)(c)}*

I I I I I I I I I I I I I I I I I I

I _____

I _____

What sound does the letter /**I**i/ make? Say it aloud.

Practice writing the lower case i on the line. The first one is an example.

i i i i i i i i i i i i i i i i i i i i i i i i

i _____

i _____

Name_____Date_____

Practice writing the Capital Letter **J** on the line. The first one is an example. *{TYS LA Pre-K to K, Pre-K LA III.C.1, III.C.2, III.C.3, IV.B.2, K 110.2(b)(5)(e), K 110.2(b)(14)(a)(b), K 110.2(b)(7)(a), K 110.2(b)(7)(c)}*

J J J J J J J J J J J J J J J J J

J _____

J _____

What sound does the letter /**Jj**/ make? Say it aloud.

Practice writing the lower case **j** on the line. The first one is an example.

j j j j j j j j j j j j j j j j j j j

j _____

j _____

Name_____Date_____

Practice writing the Capital Letter **K** on the line. The first one is an example. *{TYS LA Pre-K to K, Pre-K LA III.C.1, III.C.2, III.C.3, IV.B.2, K 110.2(b)(5)(e), K 110.2(b)(14)(a)(b), K 110.2(b)(7)(a), K 110.2(b)(7)(c)}*

K K K K K K K K K K K

K _____

K _____

What sound does the letter /**Kk**/ make? Say it aloud.

Practice writing the lower case **k** on the line. The first one is an example.

k kkkkkkkkkkkkkkkkkkkkk

k _____

k _____

Name_____Date_____

Practice writing the Capital Letter L on the line. The first one is an example. *{TYS LA Pre-K to K, Pre-K LA III.C.1, III.C.2, III.C.3, IV.B.2, K 110.2(b)(5)(e), K 110.2(b)(14)(a)(b), K 110.2(b)(7)(a), K 110.2(b)(7)(c)}*

L L L L L L L L L L L L L L

L _____

L _____

What sound does the letter /**Ll**/ make? Say it aloud.

Practice writing the lower case l on the line. The first one is an example.

l l l l l l l l l l l l l l l l l l l l l l l l l

l _____

l _____

Name_____Date_____

Practice writing the Capital Letter **M** on the line. The first one is an example. *{TYS LA Pre-K to K, Pre-K LA III.C.1, III.C.2, III.C.3, IV.B.2, K 110.2(b)(5)(e), K 110.2(b)(14)(a)(b), K 110.2(b)(7)(a), K 110.2(b)(7)(c)}*

M M M M M M M M M M
M _____

M _____

What sound does the letter /**Mm**/ make? Say it aloud.

Practice writing the lower case **m** on the line. The first one is an example.

m m m m m m m m m
m _____

m _____

Name_____ Date_____

Practice writing the Capital Letter **N** on the line. The first one is an example. *{TYS LA Pre-K to K, Pre-K LA III.C.1, III.C.2, III.C.3, IV.B.2, K 110.2(b)(5)(e), K 110.2(b)(14)(a)(b), K 110.2(b)(7)(a), K 110.2(b)(7)(c)}*

N N N N N N N N N N N

N _____

N _____

What sound does the letter /**Nn**/ make? Say it aloud.

Practice writing the lower case **n** on the line. The first one is an example.

n n n n n n n n n n n n

n _____

n _____

Name_____Date_____

Practice writing the Capital Letter O on the line. The first one is an example. *{TYS LA Pre-K to K, Pre-K LA III.C.1, III.C.2, III.C.3, IV.B.2, K 110.2(b)(5)(e), K 110.2(b)(14)(a)(b), K 110.2(b)(7)(a), K 110.2(b)(7)(c)}*

O O O O O O O O O O O

O _____

O _____

What sound does the letter /**Oo**/ make? Say it aloud.

Practice writing the lower case O on the line. The first one is an example.

o o o o o o o o o o o o

o _____

o _____

Name_____Date_____

Practice writing the Capital Letter P on the line. The first one is an example. *{TYS LA Pre-K to K, Pre-K LA III.C.1, III.C.2, III.C.3, IV.B.2, K 110.2(b)(5)(e), K 110.2(b)(14)(a)(b), K 110.2(b)(7)(a), K 110.2(b)(7)(c)}*

P P P P P P P P P P P

P _____

P _____

What sound does the letter /**Pp**/ make? Say it aloud.

Practice writing the lower case p on the line.   The first one is an example.

p p p p p p p p p p p p

p _____

p _____

Name_____Date_____

Practice writing the Capital Letter **Q** on the line. The first one
is an example. {*TYS LA Pre-K to K, Pre-K LA III.C.1, III.C.2, III.C.3, IV.B.2, K
110.2(b)(5)(e), K 110.2(b)(14)(a)(b), K 110.2(b)(7)(a), K 110.2(b)(7)(c)*}

Q Q Q Q Q Q Q Q Q Q Q

Q _____

Q _____

What sound does the letter /**Qq**/ make? Say it aloud.

Practice writing the lower case **q** on the line. The first one is an
example.

q q q q q q q q q q q q q q

q _____

q _____

Name_____Date_____

Practice writing the Capital Letter R on the line. The first one is an example. *{TYS LA Pre-K to K, Pre-K LA III.C.1, III.C.2, III.C.3, IV.B.2, K 110.2(b)(5)(e), K 110.2(b)(14)(a)(b), K 110.2(b)(7)(a), K 110.2(b)(7)(c)}*

R R R R R R R R R R R R

R _____

R _____

What sound does the letter /**Rr**/ make? Say it aloud.

Practice writing the lower case r on the line. The first one is an example.

r r r r r r r r r r r r r r

r _____

r _____

Name_____Date_____

Practice writing the Capital Letter **S** on the line. The first one is an example. *{TYS LA Pre-K to K, Pre-K LA III.C.1, III.C.2, III.C.3, IV.B.2, K 110.2(b)(5)(e), K 110.2(b)(14)(a)(b), K 110.2(b)(7)(a), K 110.2(b)(7)(c)}*

S S S S S S S S S S S

S _____

S _____

What sound does the letter /Ss/ make? Say it aloud.

Practice writing the lower case **S** on the line. The first one is an example.

S S S S S S S S S S S S S

S _____

S _____

Name_____Date_____

Practice writing the Capital Letter T on the line. The first one is an example. *{TYS LA Pre-K to K, Pre-K LA III.C.1, III.C.2, III.C.3, IV.B.2, K 110.2(b)(5)(e), K 110.2(b)(14)(a)(b), K 110.2(b)(7)(a), K 110.2(b)(7)(c)}*

T T T T T T T T T T T T T T

T _____

T _____

What sound does the letter /**Tt**/ make? Say it aloud.

Practice writing the lower case **t** on the line. The first one is an example.

t t t t t t t t t t t t t t t t t t t

t _____

t _____

Name_____Date_____

Practice writing the Capital Letter U on the line. The first one is an example. *{TYS LA Pre-K to K, Pre-K LA III.C.1, III.C.2, III.C.3, IV.B.2, K 110.2(b)(5)(e), K 110.2(b)(14)(a)(b), K 110.2(b)(7)(a), K 110.2(b)(7)(c)}*

U U U U U U U U U U U U U U U

U _____

U _____

What sound does the letter /Uu/ make? Say it aloud.

Practice writing the lower case u on the line. The first one is an example.

u u u u u u u u u u u u u u u

u _____

u _____

Name_____ Date_____

Practice writing the Capital Letter **V** on the line. The first one is an example. *{TYS LA Pre-K to K, Pre-K LA III.C.1, III.C.2, III.C.3, IV.B.2, K 110.2(b)(5)(e), K 110.2(b)(14)(a)(b), K 110.2(b)(7)(a), K 110.2(b)(7)(c)}*

V V V V V V V V V V V V V

V _____

V _____

What sound does the letter /**Vv**/ make? Say it aloud.

Practice writing the lower case **v** on the line. The first one is an example.

v v v v v v v v v v v v v

v _____

v _____

Name_____Date_____

Practice writing the Capital Letter **W** on the line. The first one is an example. *{TYS LA Pre-K to K, Pre-K LA III.C.1, III.C.2, III.C.3, IV.B.2, K 110.2(b)(5)(e), K 110.2(b)(14)(a)(b), K 110.2(b)(7)(a), K 110.2(b)(7)(c)}*

W W W W W W W W W W W

W _____

W _____

What sound does the letter /**Ww**/ make? Say it aloud.

Practice writing the lower case **w** on the line. The first one is an example.

w w w w w w w w w w w

w _____

w _____

Name_____Date_____

Practice writing the Capital Letter **X** on the line. The first one is an example. *{TYS LA Pre-K to K, Pre-K LA III.C.1, III.C.2, III.C.3, IV.B.2, K 110.2(b)(5)(e), K 110.2(b)(14)(a)(b), K 110.2(b)(7)(a), K 110.2(b)(7)(c)}*

X X X X X X X X X X X X X
_____

X _____

X _____

What sound does the letter /**Xx**/ make? Say it aloud.

Practice writing the lower case **x** on the line. The first one is an example.

x x x x x x x x x x x x x x
_____

x _____

x _____

Name_____Date_____

Practice writing the Capital Letter Y on the line. The first one is an example. *{TYS LA Pre-K to K, Pre-K LA III.C.1, III.C.2, III.C.3, IV.B.2, K 110.2(b)(5)(e), K 110.2(b)(14)(a)(b), K 110.2(b)(7)(a), K 110.2(b)(7)(c)}*

Y Y Y Y Y Y Y Y Y Y Y Y

Y _____

Y _____

What sound does the letter /**Yy**/ make? Say it aloud.

Practice writing the lower case y on the line. The first one is an example.

y y y y y y y y y y y y y

y _____

y _____

Name_____Date_____

Practice writing the Capital Letter Z on the line. The first one is
an example. *{TYS LA Pre-K to K, Pre-K LA III.C.1, III.C.2, III.C.3, IV.B.2, K
110.2(b)(5)(e), K 110.2(b)(14)(a)(b), K 110.2(b)(7)(a), K 110.2(b)(7)(c)}*

Z Z Z Z Z Z Z Z Z Z Z Z Z

Z _____

Z _____

What sound does the letter /Zz/ make? Say it aloud.

Practice writing the lower case z on the line. The first one is an
example.

z z z z z z z z z z z z z

z _____

z _____

The Young Scholar's Book Club

Name_____ Date_____

Letter Recognition

Fill in the blank with the missing letter.
{TYS LA Pre-K to K, Pre-K LA III.C.1, III.C.2, III.C.3, IV.B.2, K 110.2(b)(5)(e), K 110.2(b)(14)(a)(b), K 110.2(b)(7)(a), K 110.2(b)(7)(c)}

1. e____g   2. ____b c   3. x_____z

4. ____r s   5. w____y   6. ____e f

7. g____i   8. t____v   9. m____o

10. p ____ r

Name_____ Date_____

Letter Recognition

Circle the lower case letter that matches the Capital letter.

{TYS LA Pre-K to K, Pre-K LA III.C.1, III.C.2, III.C.3, IV.B.2, K 110.2(b)(5)(e), K 110.2(b)(14)(a)(b), K 110.2(b)(7)(a), K 110.2(b)(7)(c)}

1. A   2. K   3. R

  c d a   p k t   r s p

4. B   5. L   6. N

  d b l   q l m   s n k

7. S   8. Y

  p s z   g e y

Name_____Date_____

Beginning Sounds

Circle the letter that has the **beginning sound** of the picture. *{TYS LA Pre-K to K, Pre-K LA III.B.4, III.B.8, III.B.10, K 110.2(b)(6)(d)}*

1.   2.   3.

b c d   m t z   s g h

4.   5.   6.

k t l   p y e   a d f

7.   8.   9.

c r u   e v i   k r y

Name_____ Date_____

Beginning Sounds

Circle the letter that has the **beginning sound** of the picture. *{TYS LA Pre-K to K, Pre-K LA III.B.4, III.B.8, III.B.10, K 110.2(b)(6)(d)}*

1.   2.   3.

b c z   k r o   g v m

4.   5.   6.

o j l   a z i   f h n

7.   8.   9.

j l r   g d f   m s i

Name_____Date_____

Ending Sounds

Circle the letter that has the **ending sound** of the picture. *{TYS LA Pre-K to K, Pre-K LA III.B.4, III.B.8, III.B.10, K 110.2(b)(6)(d)}*

1.   g   p   d

2.   s   n   b

3.   k   a   t

4.   c   b   s

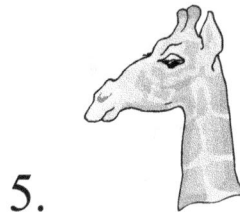

5.   g   f   k

6.   b   e   g

7.   c   m   p

8.   b   d   k

9.   f   d   k

32

Name_____ Date_____

Ending Sounds

Circle the letter that has the **ending sound** of the picture. *{TYS LA Pre-K to K, Pre-K LA III.B.4, III.B.8, III.B.10, K 110.2(b)(6)(d)}*

1.　u　k　l

2.　d　k　l

3.　n　g　f

4.　v　b　n

5.　s　k　z

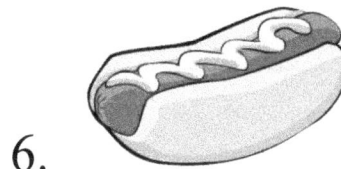

6.　h　g　i

7.　f　k　v

8.　b　l　z

9.　g　r　u

Name_____Date_____

Beginning Blends

Write the beginning blend /**ch**/ in the blank to form a word. Sound out the word. Say it aloud. {*TYS LA Pre-K to K, Pre-K LA III.B.4, III.B.7, III.B.9, IV.B.1, K 110.2(b)(6)(d)(e)(f)*}

1. _____ op

2. _____ ip

3. _____ eese

4. _____ air

5. _____ eer

6. _____ ild

7. _____urch

8. _____ in

9. _____ ick

chick

Name_____ Date_____

Beginning Blends

Write the beginning blend /**cl**/ in the blank to form a word. Sound out the word. Say it aloud. {*TYS LA Pre-K to K, Pre-K LA III.B.4, III.B.7, III.B.9, IV.B.1, K 110.2(b)(6)(d)(e)(f)*}

1. _____ock

2. _____own

3. _____ uck

4. _____ick

5. _____ap

6. _____ othes

7. _____oud

8. _____ean

clock

Name_____ Date_____

Beginning Blends

Write the beginning blend /**fl**/ in the blank to form a word. Sound out the word. Say it aloud. *{TYS LA Pre-K to K, Pre-K LA III.B.4, III.B.7, III.B.9, IV.B.1, K 110.2(b)(6)(d)(e)(f)}*

1. _____ ower

2. _____ ap

3. _____ y

4. _____ame

5. _____ag

6. _____ake

7. _____oor

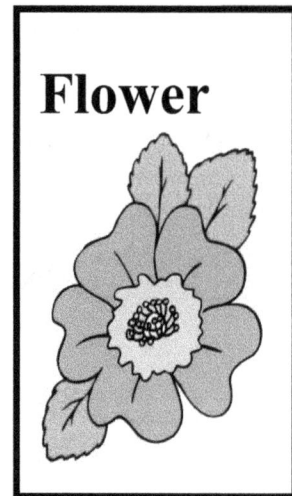

Flower

Name_____Date_____

Beginning Blends

Write the beginning blend /**sh**/ in the blank to form a word. Sound out the word. Say it aloud. {*TYS LA Pre-K to K, Pre-K LA III.B.4, III.B.7, III.B.9, IV.B.1, K 110.2(b)(6)(d)(e)(f)*}

1. _____op

2. _____ oot

3. _____ out

4. _____ irt

5. _____oe

6. _____ ower

7. _____ip

8. _____ell

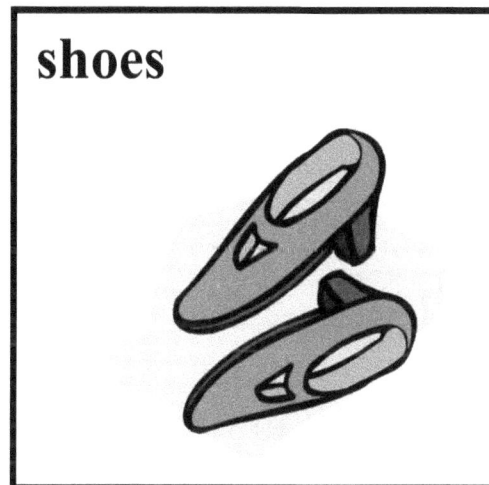

shoes

Name_____ Date_____

Ending Blends

Write the ending blend /**et**/ in the blank to form a word. Sound out the word. Say it aloud. {*TYS LA Pre-K to K, Pre-K LA III.B.4, III.B.7, III.B.9, IV.B.1, K 110.2(b)(6)(d)(e)(f)*}

1. p_____

2. l_____

3. g_____

4. m_____

5. b_____

Write /et/ in the circles below.

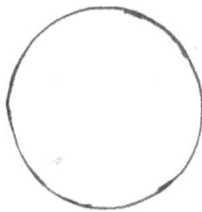

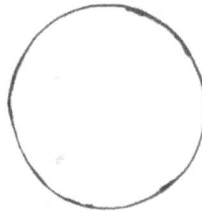

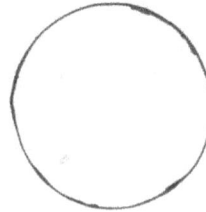

◯   ◯   ◯

Finish the sentence below.

The umbrella is w_____.

Name_____Date_____

Ending Blends

Write the ending blend /**ink**/ in the blank to form a word.
Sound out the word. Say it aloud. {*TYS LA Pre-K to K, Pre-K LA III.B.4,
III.B.7, III.B.9, IV.B.1, K 110.2(b)(6)(d)(e)(f)*}

1.shr_____

2.w_____

3.bl_____

4.s_____

5.dr_____

6.st_____

7.m_____

8.p_____

pink crayon

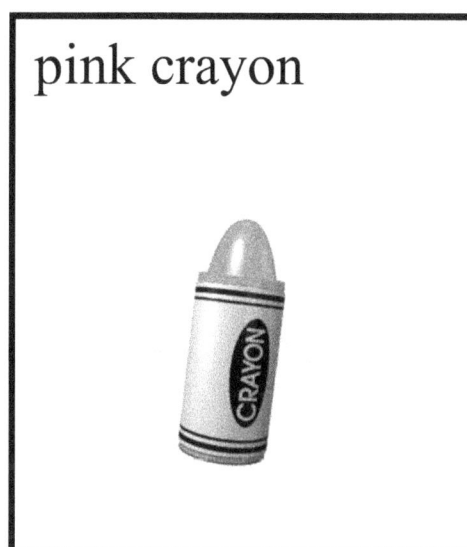

Write the correct word in the blank to complete the sentence.
Use the words from above to fill in the blanks.

1. She has a _____ coat.
2. My sister has a _____ dress.
3. The banana in the trash _____.
4. Please put the dishes in the _____.

Name_____ Date_____

Ending Blends

Write the ending blend /**at**/ in the blank to form a word. Sound out the word. Say it aloud. {*TYS LA Pre-K to K,* *Pre-K LA III.B.4, III.B.7, III.B.9, IV.B.1, K 110.2(b)(6)(d)(e)(f)*}

1. b_____

2. s_____

3. c_____

4. r_____

5. m_____

6. h _____

7. f _____

8. p_____

bat

Name_____Date_____

Ending Blends

Write the ending blend /**ug**/ in the blank to form a word. Sound out the word. Say it aloud. {*TYS LA Pre-K to K, Pre-K LA III.B.4, III.B.7, III.B.9, IV.B.1, K 110.2(b)(6)(d)(e)(f)*}

1. t_____

2. j_____

3. r_____

4. m_____

5. h_____

6. b_____

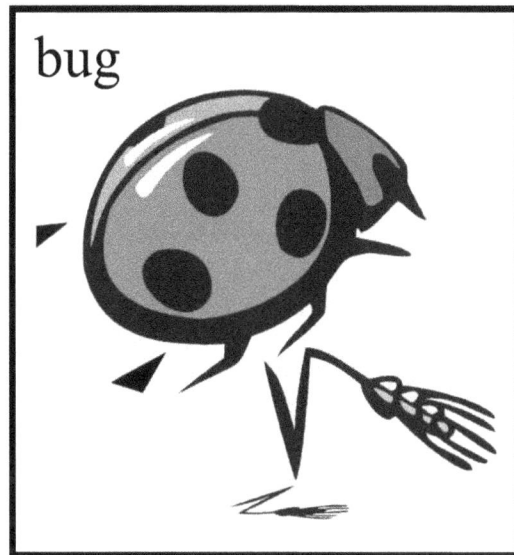

bug

Name_____Date_____

Ending Blends

Write the ending blend **/op/** in the blank to form a
word. Sound out the word. Say it aloud. {*TYS LA Pre-K to K,*
Pre-K LA III.B.4, III.B.7, III.B.9, IV.B.1, K 110.2(b)(6)(d)(e)(f)}

1. m_____

2. st_____

3. dr_____

4. ch_____

5. t_____

6. p_____

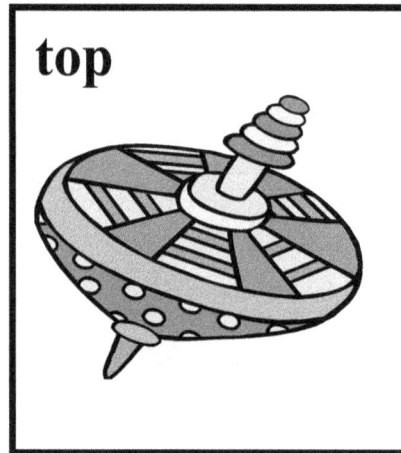

top

42

The Young Scholar's Book Club

Name_____ Date_____

Rhyming is Fun

Circle the picture that rhymes with the picture shown above. *{TYS LA Pre-K to K, Pre-K LA III.B.6, III.B.8, III.B.10, K 110.2(b)(6)(c)}*

1.

2.

3.

Name_____Date_____

It's Time To Rhyme

Circle the picture that rhymes with the picture shown above. *{TYS LA Pre-K to K, Pre-K LA III.B.6, III.B.8, III.B.10, K 110.2(b)(6)(c)}*

1.

2.

3.

Name_____ Date_____

I Know My Shapes & Colors

Color the shape with the correct color. *{TYS LA Pre-K to K}*

1. Color the rectangle blue.

2. Color the star green.

3. Color the circle red.

4. Color the diamond black.

5. Color the square brown.

Section I: Pre-K to Kindergarten

Reading

Name_____ Date_____

Title: Chicka Chicka Boom Boom
Author: Bill Martin Jr.
{TYS LA Pre-K to K, Pre-K LA III.A.1, III.A.2, III.A.3, III.D.3, K 110.2(b)(8)(a)(b)(9)(b)(10)(a)(b)}

Definitions:

1. What does Chicka Chicka Boom Boom mean to you?

   _____

2. What is a fruit? What is a vegetable?

   _____

3. Is a Coconut a fruit or a vegetable?

   _____

Questions:

1. What did A tell B?

   _____

2. Did B tell C the same thing that A told B?

   _____

3. Chicka Chicka boom boom! Will there be enough room for who in the coconut tree?

_____

4. Who tagged alone to go up the coconut tree?

_____

5. What letter comes after K?

_____

6. Can you say the next 4 letters?

_____

7. Did all the alphabets make it up the coconut tree?

_____

8. Who had a skinned-knee?

_____

9. Who had a black-eye?

_____

10. Who got out of bed after the sun went down?

_____

Name_____ Date_____

Title: This is the Way We Go to School
Author: Edith Baer
{TYS LA Pre-K to K, Pre-K LA III.A.1, III.A.2, III.A.3, III.D.3, K 110.2(b)(8)(a)(b)(9)(b)(10)(a)(b)}

Definitions:

1. Draw a picture of two flowers.

2. Draw a picture of two roller skates.   Who wears roller skates to school?

3. Draw a picture of a radio. Who goes to school by radio?

50

Questions:

1. What is the name of the child who plays on the way to school?   Where does he/she live?

2. Who goes to school by helicopter? Where does this child live?

3. Who goes to school by horse and buggy? Where does this child live?

4. Who lives in Mexico? Hawaii? China? Canada?

5. Draw a picture of the country and state you live in.

Name_____Date_____

Title: Dora's Nursery Rhyme Adventure
Author: Christine Ricci
{TYS LA Pre-K to K, Pre-K LA III.A.1, III.A.2, III.A.3, III.D.3, K 110.2(b)(8)(a)(b)(9)(b)(10)(a)(b)}

Definitions:

1. Draw a picture of Dora.

2. Draw a picture of Dora's sister and brother.

Questions:

1. What was the first nursery rhyme that Dora read to her brother and sister?

2. What problem did Dora, her brother and sister help solve in the first nursery rhyme?

3. How did Dora, her brother and sister help Humpty Dumpty?

4. What did Dora, her brother and sister do to help Old King Cole?

5. How did Dora, her brother and sister make the storm stop at the end of the story?

Name_____ Date_____

Title: Miss Tizzy
Author: Libba Moore Gray
{TYS LA Pre-K to K, Pre-K LA III.A.1, III.A.2, III.A.3, III.D.3, K 110.2 (b)(8)(a)(b)(9) (b)(10)(a)(b)

Definitions:

1. Draw a picture of Miss Tizzy's purple hat.

2. Draw a picture of Miss Tizzy's house.

Questions:

3. What did the neighbors think of Miss Tizzy?

_____

4. What is the name of Miss Tizzy's cat?

_____

5. What activities did Miss Tizzy do with the kids?

_____

6. What did Miss Tizzy do with the kids on Friday & Saturday?

_____

7. Why did the kids become sad in the story?

_____

8. What did the kids do for Miss Tizzy?

_____

9. At the end of the story what did the children do?

_____

Section I: Pre-K to Kindergarten

Mathematics

Name_____ Date_____

Practice writing the number **0** on the line below.
The first one is an example. {TYS LA Pre-K to K, Pre-K Math 1(b)(f)}

0 <u>0000000000000000000000</u>

0 _____

0 _____

0 _____

Practice writing the word **zero** on the line below.
The first one is an example.

zero <u>zero zero zero zero zero zero</u>

zero _____

zero _____

Name_____ Date_____

Practice writing the number 1 on the line below.
The first one is an example. {TYS LA Pre-K to K, Pre-K Math 1(b)(f)}

1 1 1 1 1 1 1 1 1 1 1 1 1 1 1

1 _____

1 _____

Draw 1 (one) rectangle ☐ on the line.

_____

Practice writing the word **one** on the line below.
The first one is an example.

one one one one one one one

one _____

one _____

2 The Young Scholar's Book Club

Name_____ Date_____

Practice writing the number 2 on the line below.
The first one is an example. {TYS LA Pre-K to K, Pre-K Math 1(b)(f)}

2 2 2 2 2 2 2 2 2 2 2 2 2 2 2 2 2 2 2 2

2 _____

2 _____

Draw 2 (two) triangles △ on the line.

_____

Practice writing the word two on the line below.
The first one is an example.

two two two two two two two

two _____

two _____

Name_____Date_____

Practice writing the number **3** on the line below.
The first one is an example. **{TYS LA Pre-K to K, Pre-K Math 1(b)(f)}**

3 3 3 3 3 3 3 3 3 3 3 3 3 3 3 3 3

3 _____

3 _____

Draw 3 (three) stars ☆ on the line.

_____

Practice writing the word **three** on the line below.
The first one is an example.

three three three three three

three _____

three _____

4 The Young Scholar's Book Club

Name_____ Date_____

Practice writing the number **4** on the line below.
The first one is an example. {TYS LA Pre-K to K, Pre-K Math 1(b)(f)}

4 4 4 4 4 4 4 4 4 4 4 4 4 4

4_____

4_____

Draw 4 (four) circles ◯ on the line.

_____

Practice writing the word **four** on the line below.
The first one is an example.

four four four four four four

four _____

four _____

5 The Young Scholar's Book Club

Name_____Date_____

Practice writing the number 5 on the line below.
The first one is an example. {TYS LA Pre-K to K, Pre-K Math 1(b)(f)}

5 5 5 5 5 5 5 5 5 5 5 5 5

5 _____

5 _____

Draw 5 (five) squares ☐ on the line.

_____

Practice writing the word **five** one the line below.
The first one is an example.

five five five five five five

five _____

five _____

Name_____ Date_____

Practice writing the number **6** on the line below.
The first one is an example. {TYS LA Pre-K to K, Pre-K Math 1(b)(f)}

6 6 6 6 6 6 6 6 6 6 6 6 6

6 _____

6 _____

Draw 6 (six) octagons on the line.

_____

Practice writing the word **six** on the line below.
The first one is an example.

six six six six six six six six

six _____

six _____

Name_____ Date_____

Practice writing the number 7 on the line below.
The first one is an example. {TYS LA Pre-K to K, Pre-K Math 1(b)(f)}

7 7 7 7 7 7 7 7 7 7 7 7 7 7 7

7 _____

7 _____

Draw 7 (seven) suns on the line.

_____

Practice writing the word seven on the line below.
The first one is an example.

seven seven seven seven seven

seven _____

seven _____

Name_____Date _____

Practice writing the number **8** on the line below.
The first one is an example. {TYS LA Pre-K to K, Pre-K Math 1(b)(f)}

8 8 8 8 8 8 8 8 8 8 8 8 8 8

8 _____

8 _____

Draw 8 (eight) hearts ♡ on the line.

_____

Practice writing the word **eight** on the line below.
The first one is an example.

eight eight eight eight eight

eight _____

eight _____

9   The Young Scholar's Book Club

Name_____Date_____

Practice writing the number **9** on the line below.
The first one is an example. {TYS LA Pre-K to K, Pre-K Math 1(b)(f)}

9 9 9 9 9 9 9 9 9 9 9 9 9 9

9 _____

9 _____

Draw 9 (nine) diamonds ◇ on the line.

_____

Practice writing the word **nine** on the line below.
The first one is an example.

nine   nine   nine   nine   nine   nine

nine _____

nine _____

Name_____ Date_____

Practice writing the number **10** on the line below.
The first one is an example. {TYS LA Pre-K to K, Pre-K Math 1(b)(f)}

10 10 10 10 10 10 10 10 10

10 _____

10 _____

Draw 10 (ten) ovals ◯ on the line.

_____

Practice writing the word **ten** on the line below.
The first one is an example.

ten   ten ten ten ten ten ten ten

ten _____

ten _____

The Young Scholar's Book Club

Name_____ Date_____

I Know How To Count

Circle the group with the correct amount. Take your time and count carefully. {TYS Math Pre-K to K, Pre-K Math 1(e), K 111.12(b)(1)(c)}

1. Circle 4 Bears.

2. Circle 1 bird.

I Know How To Count pg. 2

3. Circle 6 cups.

4. Circle 4 forks.

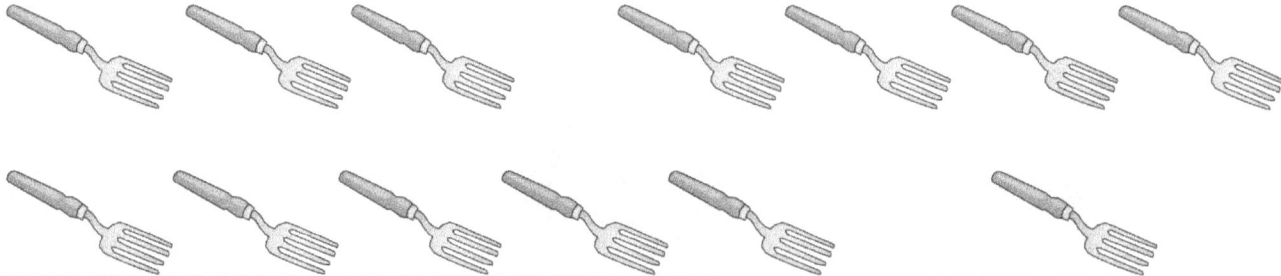

5. Circle 10 spoons.

The Young Scholar's Book Club

Name_____ Date_____

"I Can Identify My Shapes"

Find the correct match. Circle the letter that has the correct match to the shape shown above. {TYS Math Pre-K to K, Pre-K Math 3(a), K 111.12(b)(a)(c)}

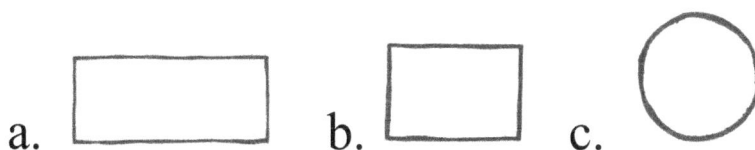

1.

a.   b.   c.

2.

a.   b.   c.

3.

a.   b.   c.

4.

a. 　　b. 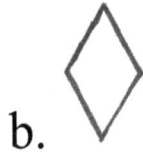　　c.

5.

a. 　　b. 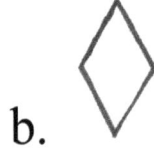　　c.

6.

a. 　　b. 　　c.

Name_____Date_____

Simple Addition

Count the pictures in each problem. How many in all?
Circle the letter that has the correct answer. {TYS Math Pre-K to K, K 111.12(b)(4)}

1. $+$ $=$

   a. 4   b. 3   c. 8

2. $+$ $=$

   a. 7   b. 9   c. 3

3. $+$ $=$

   a. 0   b. 4   c. 6

4. **+** **=**

a. 0   b. 1   c. 8

5. **+** **=**

a. 4   b. 11   c. 10

6. **+** **=**

a. 3   b. 2   c. 6

Name_____Date_____

Simple Subtraction

Count the pictures in each problem. How many are left when you remove some? Circle the letter that has the correct answer. {TYS Math Pre-K to K, K 111.12(b)(4)}

1.

a. 4   b. 1   c. 8

2.

a. 5   b. 9   c. 3

3.

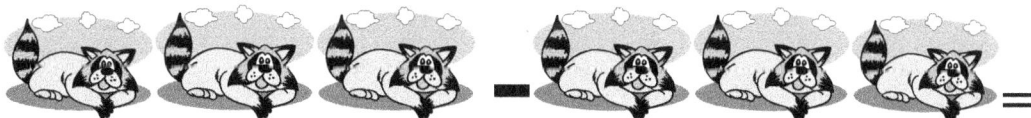

a. 0   b. 4   c. 6

4.

a. 0   b. 1   c. 4

5.

a. 3   b. 11   c. 10

6.

a. 3   b. 2   c. 6

The Young Scholar's Book Club

Name_____ Date_____

Learning to Count Money
Pennies, Nickels, & Dimes

A penny is = to 1 cent.   A nickel is = to 5 pennies.

A dime is = to 2 nickels or 10 pennies.

Count the money below? Put the Answer in the blank.
{TYS Math Pre-K to K, K 111.12(b)(4), K 111.12(b)(13)(a)(d)}

1. = _____

2. = _____

3. = _____

4. = _____

The Young Scholar's Book Club

Name_____ Date_____

Learning to Count Money
Quarters and Dollars

A Quarter is = to 5 Nickels or 25 Pennies or a

Nickel and 2 Dimes. A Dollar is =

to 4 Quarters or 20 Nickels or 100 Pennies or

4 Nickels and 8 Dimes.

Count the money below. Put the answer in the blank.

{TYS Math Pre-K to K, K 111.12(b)(4), K 111.12(b)(13)(a)(d)}

1. = _____

_____

2. = _____

_____

3. + = _____

Name_____ Date_____

Learning How To "TELL TIME"

Circle the letter that has the correct time for each clock. Look at each clock carefully. The first one is done for you. {TYS Math Pre-K to K}

1.   The answer is b. 3 o'clock

a. 2 o'clock   b. 3 o' clock   c. 6 o' clock

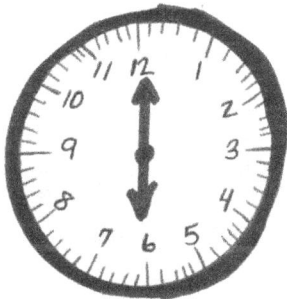

2.

a. 6 o'clock   b. 7 o' clock   c. 1 o' clock

3.

a. 2 o' clock   b. 5 o' clock   c. 9 o' clock

4.

a. 8 o' clock   b. 1 o'clock   c. 10 o' clock

5.

a. 7 o' clock   b. 3 o' clock   c. 12 o' clock

Name_____Date_____

"TELL Me The TIME"

Show the correct time. Draw the hour hand and the minute hand on each clock to show the time given in each problem.
{TYS Math Pre-K to K}

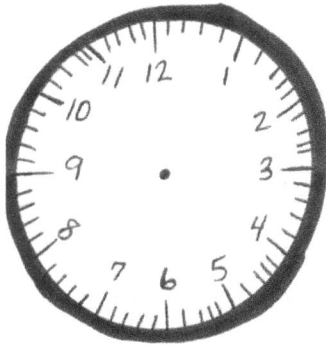

1.

3 o' clock

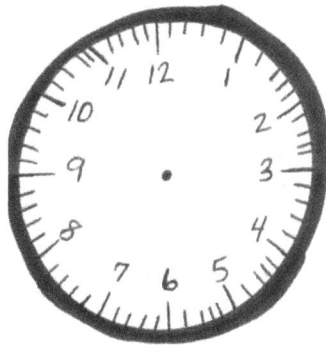

2.

7 o' clock

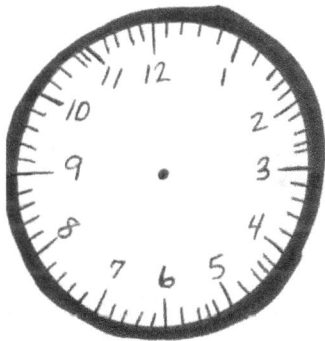

3.

9 o' clock

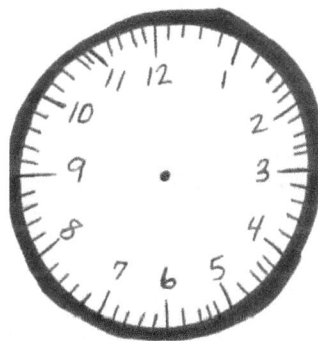

4.

1 o' clock

Name_____ Date_____

"Create Your Own Clock"

Draw your own clock. You decide what time you want on your clock. Write the numbers and draw the hour and minute hand on your clock. An example is done for you. {TYS Math Pre-K to K}

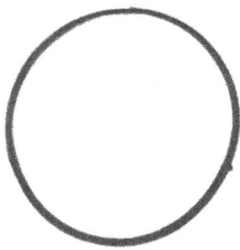

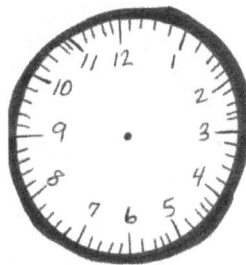

1. Start with a blank circle
2. Write your numbers
3. Draw the hour and minute hands

Name_____Date_____

Complete the Patterns

What is next in the pattern?

{TYS Math Pre-K to K, Pre-K Math 2(d), K 111.12(b)(5)(6)(a)}

1. _____

a.   b.   c.

2. _____

a.   b.   c.

3. _____

a.   b.   c.

Name_____ Date_____

Patterns are Fun to Guess

What comes next in the pattern?

{TYS Math Pre-K to K, Pre-K Math 2(d), K 111.12(b)(5)(6)(a)}

1. _____

a.   b.   c.

2. _____

a.   b.   c.

3. _____

a.   b.   c.

The Young Scholar's Book Club

Name_____Date_____

Teach Me How To Read "PICTOGRAPHS"
"The Insect and Animal Family"

4	🦋				
3	🦋		🐛		
2	🦋	🦆	🐛		🦘
1	🦋	🦆	🐛	🐌	🦘

{TYS Math Pre-K to K, Pre-K Math 5(d), K 111.12(b)(12)(a)(b)

1. How many butterflies are shown on the graph above? _____

2. How many Kangaroos are there? _____

3. How many more butterflies are there than Kangaroos?_____

4. Which animals are the same amount?_____

   How many does each animal have?_____

Name_____ Date_____

Create Your Own Graph

{TYS Math Pre-K to K, Pre-K Math 5(d), K 111.12(b)(12)(a)(b)

1. Take a blue crayon and color 4 blocks above the dog.
2. Take a purple crayon and color 1 block above the bear.
3. Take a red crayon and color 2 blocks above the frog.
4. Take a brown crayon and color 3 blocks above the chicken.
5. Take an orange crayon and color 4 blocks above the zebra.
6. Which animal has the most in its group?_____
7. Which animal has the least in its group?_____

Name_____ Date_____

Pre-Kindergarten Assessment Test

Directions to the Administrator: Give each child the 8 basic color crayons, a sharpened pencil with an eraser before starting. Please read the directions to your students for each question 2 times. Announce to students when you are starting a new section of the test. If necessary provide privacy folders for each child. The privacy folders will keep students from looking on each others assessment test. Give students enough time to finish each section. Please let your students know when it is time to begin the test.

Colors and Shapes recognition

1. Look for the rectangle shape. Color this shape yellow.

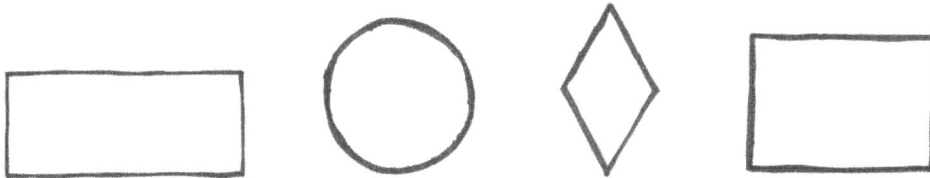

2. Look for the star shape. Color this shape red.

3. Look for the circle shape. Color this shape green.

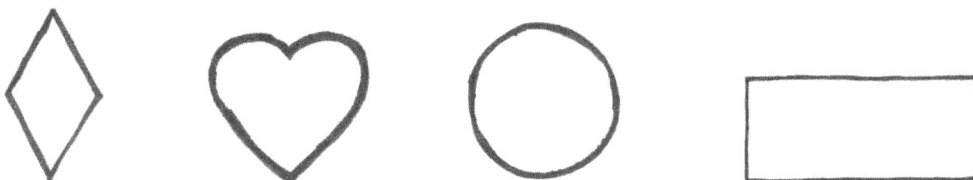

4. Look for the heart shape.   Color this shape orange.

5. Look for the diamond shape. Color this shape purple.

Letter Recognition

1. Circle the **Capital Letter** d below.

   A   C   d   G   L   D

2. Circle the **Capital Letter** k   below.

   k   Q   K   N   I   e

3. Circle the **lower case** P   below.

   b   P   l   p   U

4. Circle the **lower case** V below.

N   c   W   v   o   r

Beginning Sounds

5. Circle the picture that has the letter /d/ sound.

6. Circle the picture that has the letter /f / sound.

7. Circle the picture that has the letter /b/ sound.

8. Circle the picture that has the letter /g/ sound.

Number Recognition

1. Circle the number   8   below.

   6   9   5   4   8

2. Circle the number   10   below.

   5   11   2   10   3   5

3. Circle the number   5   below.

   9   1   5   6   0

4. Circle the number   0   below.

   0   1   8   3   12   15

5. Circle the number   13   below.

   8   9   13   11   6   2

6. Circle the number   7   below.

   9   19   2   1   7   3

Pre-Kindergarten Assessment Test pg. 5

Counting

1. How many bears are there below? Circle the correct number.

    1   6   4   7   0

2. How many fish are there below? Circle the correct number.

    8   3   2   0   1

3. How many more coats do you need to make 6. Circle the correct number.

    2   9   1   10   3

Section I: Pre-K to Kindergarten

Social Studies

Name_____ Date_____

Rules Are For Me

Definition: Rules are very important. They tell us what to do and not to do. We must follow rules everyday. We obey rules at home, at school and where ever we go. Rules help us to get along with others. Rules are given to us by our parents, teachers, and community leaders. Rules help protect us from harm and keep us safe.

Below you will see 2 (two) lists of Rules for Home and School. Look at the list and look to see what is the same and different about both lists.
{TYS Soc. St. Pre-K to K, Pre-K Soc. St. 1(c)}

Rules at HOME	Rules at SCHOOL
Don't play with fire	Play safe on the playground
Don't talk to strangers	Don't talk to strangers
Don't drink or eat harmful fluids or products.	Obey your teacher.
Obey your parents.	Walk in line down the hall

1. Draw a picture of two rules that you follow at home. You can draw an example from the chart above or another example you may have.

2. Draw a picture of someone who makes rules for you.

3. Draw a picture of what you should not do.

4. Draw a picture of your teacher and what rule you follow at school.

5. Draw a picture of a rule that you want others to follow.

Name_____Date_____

What is a Family?

Definition: A family is a group that is made up of one or two parents and all their children. (Webster's New World Children's Dictionary 2nd Ed.) {TYS Soc. St. Pre-K to K, Pre-K Soc. St. 1(a)(e)}

Your family is very important. These are the people that love and care about you. Families are made up of different people. Your family is special. No one has a family like yours.

Questions:

1. List each person that makes up your family.

2. Name 1 (one) thing that you feel is special about your family.

3. What traditions do you and your family celebrate?

4. Name something funny that happened in your family.

5. Draw a picture of your family.

Name_____Date_____

What are the 5 Senses?

In this lesson you will learn about the five senses. People have the sense of Sight, Hearing, Touch, Smell & Taste. {TYS Soc. St. Pre-K to K}

Definitions:

1. Draw a picture of an EAR.

2. Draw a picture of an EYE.

3. Draw a picture of a NOSE.

4. Draw a picture of a TONGUE.

5. Draw a picture of a HAND.

Questions:

1. Draw 3 (three) things you can see.

2. Draw 4 (four) things you can taste.

3. Draw 1 (one) thing you can hear.

4. Draw 6 (six) flowers. What body part do you use to smell the flowers?

Name_____ Date_____

Who are Community Workers?

Definition: Community workers are people who work and serve our community as police officers, trash collectors, nurses, doctors, firemen, library workers, security guards, teachers and many more.

Community workers help our communities every day. Find pictures of the community workers listed above at home or school.
{TYS Soc. St. Pre-K to K, Pre-K Soc. St. 4(b)}

Questions:

1. Draw a picture of a police officer. What does a police officer do for our community?

2. Draw a picture of a fireman. What does a fireman do for our community?

3. What do teachers do for our community?

4. Draw pictures of things that you would find in a doctor's office. What do doctors do for our community?

5. What community worker would you like to be when you finish school?

Section I: Pre-K to Kindergarten

Science

Name_____Date_____

Plants and Flowers

Plants and flowers are part of the Earth. They grow with plenty of sunlight, water and oxygen. Plants grow the foods that we eat everyday. Vegetables and fruits grow from plants. We need fruits and vegetables to help us grow and keep us healthy. People love flowers because they are beautiful. They send flowers to their family to say "I Love You." Flowers are also used to decorate many places. Animals and insects also eat plants and flowers for food to live.

{TYS Science Pre-K to K, Pre-K Science 2(d), K 112.2(b)}

1. Draw a picture of a small plant and color it.

2. Draw a picture of an apple tree and color it.

3. Draw a picture of a beautiful flower and color it.

Name_____ Date_____

The Sun and Moon

Definitions:

The Sun-- The very hot, bright star that is the center of the solar system. (Webster's New World Children's Dictionary 2nd Ed.) The sun gives light to the earth during the day. The sun also gives heat for the earth. People and plants need sunlight and heat from the sun. The heat from the sun keeps people, animals, and plants warm. The sun also help plants to grow.

The Moon—Reflects light off of the sun at night to give light to the earth. It revolves around the earth. (Webster's New World Children's Dictionary 2nd Ed.) The moon helps us to see things at night.
{TYS Science Pre-K to K, Pre-K Science 2(h), K 112.2(a)(4)(5)}

sun   **full moon**   **half moon**

1. Draw a picture of a sun in the sky and color it yellow. Color the sky blue. Label the sun.

2. Draw a picture of the moon and color it orange. Color the background black to show night time. Label the moon.

3. Why do we need the sun?   Draw three (3) things that need the sun.

4. Draw three (3) things that need the moon for light at night.

Name_____Date_____

WATER: **Water changes into 3 forms**

Materials and Books: Science books, encyclopedia or internet.

Water has the ability to change and become 3 different forms. The original form of water is a liquid. Water can also be frozen to turn into a solid. When water is boiled it turns into steam and becomes a vapor. It can be felt as moisture in the air but can not be seen.
{TYS Science Pre-K to K, Pre-K Science 1(e)(f)(h), K 112.2(a)(5)}

Experiments:

1. Take a small clear glass and fill it with water. What is the water form called in the glass? Draw a picture of a glass of water.

2. Take an ice tray and fill it with water. Place the ice tray in the freezer. Wait 2 hours. Look at the water in the ice tray. What happened to the water in the ice tray? What is the water form called in the ice tray? Draw a picture of the water form in the ice tray.

3. You will need your parents to help you on this experiment. Ask your parents to perform this project. Take a small pot and fill it half way with water. Place the small pot on the stove and turn on burner. Let the water boil in the pot. What is happening to the water? Can you see the steam in the air? What is this form of water called that is in the air above the boiling pot? Draw a picture of the boiling water in the pot.

4. Draw the 3 forms that water transforms to below:

Name_____Date_____

The Planet Earth

We live on the planet Earth. The Earth looks like a round ball in space. The Earth rotates on its axis around a star called the Sun. The Sun gives the earth light and heat.

When the Earth faces the Sun the light is called day. When the Earth rotates away from the Sun darkness falls on the Earth and it is called night.

{TYS Science Pre-K to K, Pre-K Science 2, K 112.2(a)(3)}

1. Draw your own picture of the Sun and color it.

2. Draw your own picture of the Earth and color it.

3. Show a picture of the Earth showing day time.

4. Show a picture of the Earth showing night time.

Name_____Date_____

The Scientific Method

Materials and Books: Science books, encyclopedia or internet

(Teachers, Parents, or Guardians please assist Pre-K or Kindergarten with this activity. Use a separate sheet of paper. Search the internet for Pre-K to Kindergarten science projects.)

The Scientific Method uses ordered steps to investigate a science experiment. The steps are: 1. State the question or problem 2. Research the question or problem 3. Form a Hypothesis 4. Experiment 5. Observe and take notes 6. Analyze the data 7. Draw a conclusion {TYS Science Pre-K to K, Pre-K Science 1(e)(f)(h), K 112.2(a)(5)}

Science Project:

1. State your question or problem for your science project. What do you want to find out?

2. Research your question or problem. You can go to the library to check out books on your question or problem. Search the internet, encyclopedias, science books or interview professionals on your subject.

3. After you do your research write a Hypothesis. A Hypothesis is an educated guess. What do you think will be the outcome of your problem or question?

4. It is now time to test your Hypothesis. Do an experiment. Gather the materials you need to do your experiment. Write a list of everything you used in the experiment. Write down the steps you followed to perform your experiment.

5. During the experiment make sure you write down what happens. What did you see, smell, hear, or observe?

6. Now take your notes and analyze what you wrote in your notes. Analyze what happened in the experiment. Analyze means to look at every detail, write down the causes and effects of the details and write the results.

7. Draw a Conclusion. Write down your result or answer for your problem or question. What was the final result? Did you predict the correct answer for your Hypothesis?

Section I: Pre-K to Kindergarten

Answer Key

Pre-K to Kindergarten Language Arts Key

Letters Aa to Ss

Handwriting will vary.

Letters Tt to Zz

Handwriting will vary.

The Young Scholar's Book Club

Name_____ Date_____

Letter Recognition

Fill in the missing letter in the alphabet pattern.
*(TYS LA Pre-K to K, Pre-K LA III.C.1, III.C.2, III.C.3, IV.B.2, & 110.2(b)(5)(ii),
K 110.2(b)(1)(A)(iii)(bk), K 110.2(b)(7)(iA), K 110.2(b)(7)(ii))*

1. e **f** g   2. **a** bc   3. x **y** z

4. **q** rs   5. w **x** y   6. **d** ef

7. g **h** i   8. t **u** v   9. m **n** o

10. p **q** r

The Young Scholar's Workbook: Book 1, Vol. 1 www.tysbookclub.com

---

The Young Scholar's Book Club

Name_____ Date_____

Letter Recognition

Circle the lower case letter that matches the Capital letter.
*(TYS LA Pre-K to K, Pre-K LA III.C.1, III.C.2, III.C.3, IV.B.2, & 110.2(b)(5)(ii),
K 110.2(b)(1)(A)(iii)(bk), K 110.2(b)(7)(ii))*

1. A   2. K   3. R
c d (a)   p (k) t   (r) s p

4. B   5. I   6. N
d (b) f   q (I) m   s (n) k

7. S   8. Y
p (s) z   g c (y)

The Young Scholar's Workbook: Book 1, Vol. 1 www.tysbookclub.com

---

The Young Scholar's Book Club

Name_____ Date_____

Beginning Sounds

Circle the letter that represents the **beginning sound**
of the picture. *(TYS LA Pre-K to K, Pre-K LA III.B.4, III.B.8, III.B.10,
K 110.2(b)(9)(ii))*

1.   2.   3.
b c (d)   m (t) z   (w) g h

4.   5.   6.
k (t) i   (p) y e   (s) d f

7.   8.   9.
(c) r u   (p) v i   k (p) y

The Young Scholar's Workbook: Book 1, Vol. 1 www.tysbookclub.com

---

The Young Scholar's Book Club

Name_____ Date_____

Beginning Sounds

Circle the letter that represents the **beginning sound**
of each picture. *(TYS LA Pre-K to K, Pre-K LA III.B.4, III.B.8, III.B.10,
K 110.2(b)(9)(ii))*

1.   2.   3.
(b) c z   k (p) o   g v (m)

4.   5.   6.
(c) j l   a (z) i   (h) h n

7.   8.   9.
j l (r)   (g) d f   m (s) i

The Young Scholar's Workbook: Book 1, Vol. 1 www.tysbookclub.com

---

The Young Scholar's Book Club

Name_____ Date_____

Ending Sounds

Circle the letter that represents the **ending sound** of
each picture. *(TYS LA Pre-K to K, Pre-K LA III.B.4, III.B.8, III.B.10,
K 110.2(b)(9)(ii))*

1.   2.   3.
(g) p d   s (n) b   k a (t)

4.   5.   6.
c b (s)   g (f) k   b (g) d

7.   8.   9.
e m (p)   (b) d k   f d (k)

The Young Scholar's Workbook: Book 1, Vol. 1 www.tysbookclub.com

---

The Young Scholar's Book Club

Name_____ Date_____

Ending Sounds

Circle the letter that represents the **ending sound** of
each picture. *(TYS LA Pre-K to K, Pre-K LA III.B.4, III.B.8, III.B.10,
K 110.2(b)(9)(ii))*

1.   2.   3.
u k (l)   d (k) l   n g (t)

4.   5.   6.
v b (n)   s k z   h (t) i

7.   8.   9.
f (k) v   b (l) z   g r u

The Young Scholar's Workbook: Book 1, Vol. 1 www.tysbookclub.com

---

ch The Young Scholar's Book Club

Name_____ Date_____

Beginning Blends

Write the beginning blend /ch/ in the blank to form a
word. Sound out the word. Say it aloud. *(TYS LA Pre-K to J,
Pre-K LA III.B.4, III.B.7, III.B.9, IV.B.1, K 110.2(b)(6)(i)(p)(5)(E))*

1. **Ch** op

2. **Ch** ip

3. **Ch** eese

4. **Ch** air

5. **Ch** eer

6. **Ch** ild

7. **Ch** urch

8. **Ch** in

9. **Ch** ick

chick

The Young Scholar's Workbook: Book 1, Vol. 1 www.tysbookclub.com

Name_____ Date_____

Beginning Blends

Write the beginning blend /cl/ in the blank to form a word. Sound out the word. Say it aloud. *(TYS LA Pre-K to K Pre-K LA III.B.4, III.B.7, III.B.9, IV.B.1, & 110.2(b)(4)(b)(c)(f))*

1. __cl__ ock
2. __cl__ own
3. __cl__ uck
4. __cl__ ick
5. __cl__ ap
6. __cl__ othes
7. __cl__ oud
8. __cl__ ean

clock

Name_____ Date_____

Beginning Blends

Write the beginning blend /fl/ in the blank to form a word. Sound out the word. Say it aloud. *(TYS LA Pre-K to K, Pre-K LA III.B.4, III.B.7, III.B.9, IV.B.1, & 110.2(b)(4)(b)(c)(f))*

1. __fl__ ower
2. __fl__ ap
3. __fl__ y
4. __fl__ ame
5. __fl__ ag
6. __fl__ ake
7. __fl__ oor

Flower

Name_____ Date_____

Beginning Blends

Write the beginning blend /sh/ in the blank to form a word. Sound out the word. Say it aloud. *(TYS LA Pre-K to K. Pre-K LA III.B.4, III.B.7, III.B.9, IV.B.1, & 110.2(b)(4)(b)(c)(f))*

1. __Sh__ op
2. __Sh__ oot
3. __Sh__ out
4. __Sh__ irt
5. __Sh__ oe
6. __Sh__ ower
7. __Sh__ ip
8. __Sh__ ell

shoes

Name_____ Date_____

Ending Blends

Write the ending blend /et/ in the blank to form a word. Sound out the word. Say it aloud. *(TYS LA Pre-K to K, Pre-K LA III.B.4, III.B.7, III.B.9, IV.B.1, & 110.2(b)(4)(b)(c)(f))*

1. p__et__
2. l__et__
3. g__et__
4. m__et__
5. b__et__

Write /et/ in the circles below.

(et) (et) (et)

Finish the sentence below with /et/ in the blank.

The umbrella is w__et__

Name_____ Date_____

Ending Blends

Write the ending blend /ink/ in the blank to form a word. Sound out the word. Say it aloud. *(TYS LA Pre-K to K, Pre-K LA III.B.4, III.B.7, III.B.9, IV.B.1, & 110.2(b)(4)(b)(c)(f))*

1. shr__ink__
2. w__ink__
3. bl__ink__
4. s__ink__
5. dr__ink__
6. st__ink__
7. m__ink__
8. p__ink__

pink crayon

Write the correct word in the blank to complete the sentence. Use the words from above to fill in the blanks.
1. She has a __mink__ coat.
2. My sister has a __pink__ dress.
3. The banana in the trash __stink__
4. Please put the dishes in the __sink__

Name_____ Date_____

Ending Blends

Write the ending blend /at/ in the blank to form a word. Sound out the word. Say it aloud. *(TYS LA Pre-K to K, Pre-K LA III.B.4, III.B.7, III.B.9, IV.B.1, & 110.2(b)(4)(b)(c)(f))*

1. b__at__
2. s__at__
3. c__at__
4. r__at__
5. m__at__
6. h__at__
7. f__at__
8. p__at__

bat

Name_____ Date_____

Ending Blends

Write the ending blend /ug/ in the blank to form a word. Sound out the word. Say it aloud. *(TYS LA Pre-K to K, Pre-K LA III.B.4, III.B.7, III.B.9, IV.B.1, & 110.2(b)(4)(b)(c)(f))*

1. t__ug__
2. j__ug__
3. r__ug__
4. m__ug__
5. h__ug__
6. b__ug__

bug

Name_____ Date_____

Ending Blends

Write the ending blend /op/ in the blank to form a word. *(TYS LA Pre-K to K, Pre-K LA III.B.4, III.B.7, III.B.9, IV.B.1, & 110.2(b)(4)(b)(c)(f))*

1. m__op__
2. st__op__
3. dr__op__
4. ch__op__
5. t__op__
6. p__op__

top

Name_____ Date_____

I Know My Shapes & Colors

Color the picture with the correct color. *(TYS LA Pre-K to K)*

1. Color the rectangle blue.

2. Color the star green.

3. Color the circle red.

4. Color the diamond black.

5. Color the square brown.

Pre-K to Kindergarten Language Arts Key

Name_____ Date_____

Rhyming is Fun

Circle the picture that rhymes with the picture listed above. *[TYS LA Pre-K to K, Pre-K LA III.B.6, III.B.8, III.B.10, K 110.2(6c)(C I]*

1.
2.
3.

The Young Scholar's Workbook: Book 1, Vol. 1 www.tysbookclub.com

---

Name_____ Date_____

It's Time To Rhyme

Circle the picture that rhymes with the picture listed above. *[TYS LA Pre-K to K, Pre-K LA III.B.6, III.B.8, III.B.10, K 110.2(6)(9) c I]*

1.
2.
3.

The Young Scholar's Workbook: Book 1, Vol. 1 www.tysbookclub.com

---

Name_____ Date_____

Title: Chicka Chicka Boom Boom
Author: Bill Martin Jr.
[TYS LA Pre-K to K, Pre-K LA III.A.1, III.A.2, III.A.3, III.D.3, K 110.2(b)(3)(a)(4)(a)(6a)(6b)(6c)]

Definitions:

1. What do you think Chicka Chicka Boom Boom mean?
   Answers will vary

2. What is a fruit? What is a vegetable?
   ovary seed plant used for food.
   a plants seed, roots, leaves used for food.

3. Is a Coconut a fruit or a vegetable?
   fruit

Questions:

1. What did A tell B?
   I will meet you at the top of the Coconut tree!

2. Did B tell C the same thing that A told B?
   yes

48

---

3. Chicka Chicka boom boom! Will there be enough room for who in the coconut tree?
   H

4. Who tagged alone to go up the coconut tree?
   K

5. What letter comes after K?
   L

6. Can you say the next 4 letters?
   MNOP

7. Did all the alphabets make it up the coconut tree?
   YES

8. Who had a skinned-knee?
   D

9. Who had a black-eye?
   P

10. Who got out of bed after the sun went down?
    A

49

Name_____ Date_____

Title: This is the Way We Go to School
Author: Edith Baer
[TYS LA Pre-K to K, Pre-K LA I.I III.A.1, III.A.2, III.A.3, K 110.2(b)(6a)(6b)(6c)(6d)]

Definitions:

1. Draw a picture of two flowers
   Pictures will vary

2. Draw a picture of two roller skates. Who wears roller skates to school?
   Pictures will vary.
   The Student with yellow shirt + poca dots

3. Draw a picture of a radio. Who goes to school by radio?
   Pictures will vary.
   Kay, Fay, Flo, Joe

50

Questions:

1. What is the name of the child who plays on the way to school? Where does he/she live?
   Mira, She lives in Isreal.

2. Who goes to school by helicopter? Where does this child live?
   Students who live in Siberia, U.S.S.R.

3. Who goes to school by horse and buggy? Where does this child live?
   Jake + Jane
   Lancaster, Pennsylvania, U.S.A.

4. Who lives in Mexico? Hawaii? China? Canada?
   Carlos + Luz, Ellen lives in Hawaii, Mei + Ling live in China, Skidoo Passengers live in Canada.

5. Draw a picture of the country and state you live in.
   Pictures will vary.

51

Name_____ Date_____

Title: Dora's Nursery Rhyme Adventure
Author: Christine Ricci
[TYS LA Pre-K to K, Pre-K LA A.1, III.A.2, III.A.3, III.D.3, K 110.2(b)(6a)(6b)(6c)(6d)(6e)]

Definitions:

1. Draw a picture of Dora.
   Pictures will vary

2. Draw a picture of Dora's sister and brother.
   Pictures will vary

Questions:

1. What was the first nursery rhyme that Dora read to her brother and sister?
   Jack + Jill

2. What problem did Dora, her brother and sister help solve in the first nursery rhyme? get back up hill

52

---

3. How did Dora, her brother and sister help Humpty Dumpty? They put pillows down around the wall so Humpty would not get hurt.

4. What did Dora, her brother and sister do to help Old King Cole? They helped him find his bowl, three fiddlers and his pipe.

5. How did Dora, her brother and sister make the storm stop at the end of the story? They began to sing rain rain go away come again some other day. The storm cloud went away.

53

116

Pre-K to Kindergarten Reading & Mathematics Key

The Young Scholar's Book Club

Name_____ Date_____

Title: Miss Tizzy
Author: Libba Moore Gray
[TYS L.4 Pre-K to K, Pre-K L.3 (II.A.1, III.A.2, III.A.3, III.D.3, & 179.2 (la(B)(scii)(9) (b) (1)(sis)(9)]

Definitions:

1. Draw a picture of Miss Tizzy's purple hat.

Drawings Will Vary

2. Draw a picture of Miss Tizzy's house.

Drawings Will Vary

Questions:

3. What did the neighbors think of Miss Tizzy?

She was peculiar

4. What is the name of Miss Tizzy's cat?

Hiram

5. What activities did Miss Tizzy do with the kids?

baked cookies, puppet show, skating, draw pictures, sang songs, dress up

6. What did Miss Tizzy do with the kids on Friday & Saturday?

dress up and skating

7. Why did the kids become sad in the story?

Miss Tizzy was sick

8. What did the kids do for Miss Tizzy?

baked cookies, puppet show, sang songs, gave her skates, tea and pictures, played drums.

9. At the end of the story what did the children do?

Sang moon songs under her window.

Numbers 0-10

Handwriting will vary.

The Young Scholar's Book Club

Name_____ Date_____

I Know How To Count

Find the group with the correct amount. Take your time and count carefully. [TYS Math Pre-K to K, Pre-K Math 1(a), K 11.12(B)(1)(3)]

1. Circle 4 Bears.

2. Circle 1 bird.

I Know How To Count pg. 2

3. Circle 6 cups.

4. Circle 4 forks.

5. Circle 10 spoons.

The Young Scholar's Book Club

Name_____ Date_____

"I Can Identify My Shapes"

Match the shapes below. Circle the correct answer that matches the shape in each problem. [TYS Math Pre-K to K, Pre-K Math A(a), K 111.1D(b)(a)(v Q]

1.

2.

3.

4.

5.

6.

The Young Scholar's Book Club

Name_____ Date_____

Simple Addition

Count the objects in each problem. How many in all? Circle the number that shows the correct answer.
[TYS Math Pre-K to K, K 111.12(b)(4)]

1. a. 4   b. 3   c. 8

2. a. 7   b. 9   c. 3

3. a. 0   b. 4   c. 6

---

4. a. 0   b. 1   c. 8

5. a. 4   b. 11   c. 10

6. a. 3   b. 2   c. 6

Name_____ Date_____

Simple Subtraction

Count the objects in each problem. How many are left when you remove some objects? Circle the number that shows the correct answer. {TYS Math Pre-K to K, K 111.12(b)(6)}

1.

a. 4   (b) 1   c. 8

2.

a. 5   b. 9   (c) 3

3.

(a) 0   b. 4   c. 6

The Young Scholar's Workbook: Book 1, Vol. 1 www.tysbookclub.com

---

4.

a. 0   b. 1   (c) 4

5.

(a) 3   b. 11   c. 10

6.

a. 3   (b) 2   c. 6

The Young Scholar's Workbook: Book 1, Vol. 1 www.tysbookclub.com

---

Name_____ Date_____

Learning to Count Money
Pennies, Nickels, & Dimes

A penny is = to 1 cent.   A nickel is = to 5 pennies.

A dime is = to 2 nickels or 10 pennies.

Count How Much Money? Put the Answer in the blank
{TYS Math Pre-K to K, K 111.12(b)(4); K 111.15(b)(3)(c)(1)}

1. 4¢

2. 20¢

3. 15¢

4. 2¢

The Young Scholar's Workbook: Book 1, Vol. 1 www.tysbookclub.com

---

Name_____ Date_____

Learning to Count Money
Quarters and Dollars

A Quarter is = to 5 Nickels or 25 Pennies or a Nickel and 2 Dimes. A Dollar is = to 4 Quarters or 20 Nickels or 100 Pennies or 4 Nickels and 8 Dimes.

Count the money below. Put the answer in the blank.
{TYS Math Pre-K to K, K 111.12(b)(4); K 111.15(b)(3)(c)(1)}

1. $2.00

2. 75¢

3. $1.50

The Young Scholar's Workbook: Book 1, Vol. 1 www.tysbookclub.com

---

Name_____ Date_____

Learning How To "TELL TIME"

Circle the right time below each clock. Look at each clock carefully. The first one is done for you.
{TYS Math Pre-K to K}

1. The answer is b. 3 o'clock.

a. 2 o'clock   (b) 3 o'clock   c. 6 o'clock

2.

(a) 6 o'clock   b. 7 o'clock   c. 1 o'clock

The Young Scholar's Workbook: Book 1, Vol. 1 www.tysbookclub.com

---

3.

a. 2 o'clock   (b) 5 o'clock   c. 9 o'clock

4.

a. 8 o'clock   (b) 1 o'clock   c. 10 o'clock

5.

a. 7 o'clock   b. 3 o'clock   (c) 12 o'clock

The Young Scholar's Workbook: Book 1, Vol. 1 www.tysbookclub.com

---

Name_____ Date_____

"TELL Me The TIME"

Label each blank clock below with the right time. Draw the hour hand and the minute hand on each clock to display the time given in each problem. {TYS Math Pre-K to K}

1. 3 o'clock

2. 7 o'clock

3. 9 o'clock

4. 1 o'clock

Name_____ Date_____

"Create Your Own Clock"

Draw your own clock and label it. You decide what time you want on your clock. Label the numbers and draw the hour and minute hand on your clock. An example is done for you. {TYS Math Pre-K to K}

1. Start with a blank circle
2. Label your numbers
3. Draw the hour and minute hands

Drawings Will Vary

The Young Scholar's Workbook: Book 1, Vol. 1 www.tysbookclub.com

---

Name_____ Date_____

Complete the Patterns

What is next in the pattern?
{TYS Math Pre-K to K, Pre-K Math 2(d), K 111.12(b)(5)(a)(aa)}

1. a.   (b)   c.

2. a.   (b)   c.

3. a.   (b)   c.

The Young Scholar's Workbook: Book 1, Vol. 1 www.tysbookclub.com

---

Name_____ Date_____

Patterns are Fun to Guess

What comes next in the pattern?
[TYS Math Pre-K to K, Pre-K Math 2nd, K J11.12bhe5jcmd]

1.

a. b. c.

2.

a. b. c.

3.

a. b. c.

Name_____ Date_____

Teach Me How To Read "PICTOGRAPHS"
"The Insect and Animal Family"

4	🦋		
3	🦋	🐝	
2	🦋	🐝	🦘
1	🦋	🐝	🦘

[TYS Math Pre-K to K, Pre-K Math Std's K J11.12bhe12jcmb]

1. How many butterflies are shown on the graph above? **4**

2. How many Kangaroos are there? **2**

3. How many more butterflies are there than Kangaroos? **2**

4. Which animals are the same amount? **Ducks Kangaroos**
How many does each animal have? **2**

5. How many bees are there? **3**

Name_____ Date_____

Create Your Own Graph
[TYS Math Pre-K to K, Pre-K Math Std's K J11.12bhe12jcmb]

1. Take a blue crayon and color 4 blocks above the dog.
2. Take a purple crayon and color 1 block above the bear.
3. Take a red crayon and color 2 blocks above the frog.
4. Take a brown crayon and color 3 blocks above the chicken.
5. Take an orange crayon and color 4 blocks above the zebra.
6. Which animal has the most in its group? **Zebra, Dog**
7. Which animal has the least in its group? **Bear**
8. What two animals have the same in their group? **Zebra, Dog**

Name_____ Date_____

Pre-Kindergarten Assessment Test

Directions to the Administrator: Give each child the 8 basic color crayons, a sharpened pencil with an eraser before starting. Please read the directions to your students for each question 2 times. Announce to students when you are starting a new section of the test. If necessary provide privacy folders for each child. The privacy folders will keep students from looking on each others assessment test. Please let your students know when it is time to begin the test.

Colors and Shapes recognition

1. Look for the rectangle shape. Color this shape yellow.

2. Look for the star shape. Color this shape red.

3. Look for the circle shape. Color this shape green.

Pre-Kindergarten Assessment Test pg. 2

4. Look for the heart shape. Color this shape orange.

5. Look for the diamond shape. Color this shape purple.

Letter Recognition

1. Circle the **Capital Letter** d below.

A   C   d   G   L   (D)

2. Circle the **Capital Letter** k below.

k   Q   (K)   N   I   e

3. Circle the **lower case** P below.

h   P   I   (p)   U

Pre-Kindergarten Assessment Test pg. 3

4. Circle the **lower case** V below.

N   c   W   (v)   o   r

Beginning Sounds

5. Circle the animal that has the letter /d/ sound.

6. Circle the animal that has the letter /f/ sound.

7. Circle the picture that has the letter /b/ sound.

8. Circle the picture that has the letter /g/ sound.

Pre-Kindergarten Assessment Test pg. 4

Number Recognition

1. Circle the number 8 below.

6   9   5   4   (8)

2. Circle the number 10 below.

5   11   (10)   3   5

3. Circle the number 5 below.

9   1   (5)   6   0

4. Circle the number 0 below.

(0)   1   8   3   12   15

5. Circle the number 13 below.

8   9   (13)   11   6   2

6. Circle the number 7 below.

9   19   2   1   (7)   3

Pre-Kindergarten Assessment Test pg. 5

Counting

1. How many bears are there below? Circle the correct number.

1   6   (4)   7   0

2. How many fish are there below? Circle the correct number.

8   3   (2)   0   1

3. How many more coats do you need to make 6. Circle the correct number.

2   9   1   10   (3)

Pre-K to Kindergarten Social Studies & Science Key

The Young Scholar's Book Club

Name_____ Date_____

Rules Are For Me

Definition: Rules are very important. They tell us what to do and not to do. We must follow rules everyday. We obey rules at home, at school and where ever we go. Rules help us to get along with others. Rules are given to us by our parents, teachers, and other adults. Rules help protect us from harm and keep us safe.

Below you will see 2 (two) lists of Rules for Home and School. Look at the list and look to see what is the same and different about both lists. (TYS Soc. St. Pre-K to K, Pre-K Soc. St. 1t 1)

Rules at HOME	Rules at SCHOOL
Don't play with fire	Play safe on the playground
Don't talk to strangers	Don't talk to strangers
Don't drink or eat harmful fluids or products.	Obey your teachers
Obey your parents	Walk in line down the hall

1. Draw a picture of two rules that you follow at home. You can draw an example from the chart above or another example you may have.

Drawings Will Vary

---

2. Draw a picture of someone who makes rules for you.

Drawings Will Vary

3. Draw a picture of what you should not do.

Drawings Will Vary

4. Draw a picture of your teacher and what rule you follow at school.

Drawings will vary

---

5. Draw a picture of a rule that you want others to follow.

Drawings Will Vary

The Young Scholar's Book Club

Name_____ Date_____

What is a Family?

Definition: A family is a group that is made up of one or two parents and all their children. (Webster's New World Children's Dictionary 2nd Ed.) (TYS Soc. St. Pre-K to K, Pre-K 11&&0)

Your family is very important. These are the people that love and care about you. Families are made up of different people. Your family is special. No one has a family like yours.

Questions:

1. List each person that makes up your family.

answers will vary

2. Name 1 (one) thing that you feel is special about your family.

answers will vary

3. What traditions do you and your family celebrate?

answers will vary

---

4. Name something funny that happened in your family.

answers will vary

5. Draw a picture of your family

Drawings Will Vary

The Young Scholar's Book Club

Name_____ Date_____

What are the 5 Senses?

In this lesson you will learn about the five senses. People have the sense of Sight, Hearing, Touch, Smell & Taste. (TYS Soc. St. Pre-K to K)

Definitions:

1. Draw a picture of an EAR *example*

2. Draw a picture of an EYE *example*

3. Draw a picture of a NOSE *example*

4. Draw a picture of a TONGUE *example*

---

5. Draw a picture of a HAND *example*

Questions:

1. Draw 3 (three) things you can see.

Drawings Will Vary

2. Draw 4 (four) things you can taste.

Drawings Will Vary

3. Draw 1 (one) thing you can hear.

drawings will vary

4. Draw 6 (six) flowers. What body part do you use to smell the flowers? *nose*

The Young Scholar's Book Club

Name_____ Date_____

Who are Community Workers?

Definition: Community worker are people who work and serve our community as police officers, trash collectors, nurses, doctors, firemen, library workers, security guards, teachers, and many more.

Community workers help our communities every day. Find pictures of the community workers listed above at home or school. (TYS Soc. St. Pre-K to K, Pre-K Soc. St. 4&b)

Questions:

1. Draw a picture of a police officer. What does a police officer do for our community?

Drawings will vary. Protect us.

2. Draw a picture of a fireman. What does a fireman do for our community?

Drawings will vary. Put out fires.

---

3. What do teachers do for our community?

teach children

4. Draw pictures of things that you would find in a doctor's office. What do doctors do for our community?

Drawings will vary. Take care of sick people.

5. What community worker would you like to be when you finish school?

Drawings will vary

Name_____ Date_____

Plants & Flowers

Plants and flowers are part of the Earth. They grow with plenty of sunlight and oxygen. Plants grow the foods that we eat everyday. Vegetables and fruits grow from plants. We need fruits and vegetables to help us grow and keep us healthy. People love flowers because they are beautiful. They send flowers to their family to say "I Love You." Flowers are also used to decorate many places. Animals and insects also eat plants and flowers for food to live.

[TYS Science Pre-K to K, Pre-K Science 2(d), K 112.2(6b)]

1. Draw a picture of a small plant and color it.

2. Draw a picture of an apple tree and color it.

3. Draw a picture of a beautiful flower and color it.

Name_____ Date_____

The Sun & Moon

Definitions:

The Sun -- The very hot, bright star that is the center of the solar system. (Webster's New World Children's Dictionary 2nd Ed.) The sun gives light to the earth during the day. The sun also gives heat for the earth. People and plants need sunlight and heat from the sun. The heat from the sun keeps people, animals, and plants warm. The sun also helps plants to grow.

The Moon—Reflects light off of the sun at night to give light to the earth. It revolves around the earth. (Webster's New World Children's Dictionary 2nd Ed.) The moon helps us to see things at night.
[TYS Science Pre-K to K, Pre-K Science 2(b), K 112.2(a)(4a5)]

sun   full moon   half moon

1. Draw a picture of a sun in the sky and color it yellow. Color the sky blue. Label the sun.

Sun

---

2. Draw a picture of the moon and color it orange. Color the background black to show night time. Label the moon.

moon

3. Why do we need the sun? Draw three (3) things that need the sun.

for light
heat
help plants grow
Drawings will vary

4. Draw three (3) things that need the moon for light at night.

Drawings will vary

Name_____ Date_____

WATER: Water changes into 3 forms

Materials and Books: Science books or encyclopedia on water.

Water has the ability to change and become 3 different forms. The original form of water is a liquid. Water can also be frozen to turn into a solid. When water is boiled it turns into steam and becomes a vapor. It can be felt as moisture in the air but can not be seen.
[TYS Science Pre-K to K, Pre-K Science 11(a)(5a)(b), K 112.2(a)(5j)]

Experiments:

1. Take a small clear glass and fill it with water. What is the water form called in the glass? Draw a picture of a glass of water.

liquid   water

---

2. Take an ice tray and fill it with water. Place the ice tray in the freezer. Wait atleast 2 hours. Look at the water in the ice tray. What happened to the water in the ice tray? What is the water form called in the ice tray? Draw a picture of the water form in the ice tray.

The water froze. The water form is ice.

3. You will need your parents to help you on this experiment. Ask your parents to perform this project. Take a small pot and fill it half way with water. Place the small pot on the stove and turn on burner. Let the water boil in the pot. What is happening to the water? Can you see the steam in the air? What is this form of water called that is in the air above the boiling pot? Draw a picture of the boiling water in the pot.

The water is boiling. It is evaporating in the air. It is called steam.

4. Draw the 3 forms that water transforms to below.

water liquid   ice cubes   steam

Name_____ Date_____

The Planet Earth

We live on the planet Earth. The Earth looks like a round ball in space. The Earth circles around a star called the Sun. The Sun gives the earth light and heat.

When the Earth faces the Sun the light is called day. When the Earth circles away from the Sun darkness falls on the Earth and it is called night.
[TYS Science Pre-K to K, Pre-K Science 2, K 112.2(a)(3)]

1. Draw your own picture of the Sun and color it.

2. Draw your own picture of the Earth and color it.

---

3. Show a picture of the Earth showing day time.

earth   sun

4. Show a picture of the Earth showing night time.

earth   moon

Scientific Method

Science Projects will vary.

Scientific Method

Science Projects will vary.

Table of Contents
Section II: 1st to 4th Grade

Science 173

Writing 183

Section II: 1st to 4th Grade

Language Arts

Name_____ Date_____

Noun? What is a noun?

(a.) an action word (b.) a person, place, or thing. (c.) a descriptive word

If you chose answer (b) you are correct. A noun is a person, place, or thing. Examples of some nouns are: Mr. Samson, The Grand Canyon, Lucy, toys
Mr. Samson is a person, The Grand Canyon is a place, Lucy is a person, and toys are things.

In the activity below underline all the nouns in each sentence. After you underline the nouns label each with a letter N. **{TYS LA 1st to 4th, 1 110.3(a)(1)(4), 2 110.4(b)(3)(e), 2 110.4(a), 3 110.5(a)(4), 4 110.6(a)(4)}**

The first sentence is done for you.

1. The <u>woman</u> went to the <u>store</u> to buy a <u>coat.</u>
       N   N   N

2. Yellow Stone Park is a great place to visit.

3. The dog ran across the street.

4. The silver watch is pretty.

5. Mother Goose is a fairytale character.

6. The black truck raced down the freeway.

7. My blue folder is on the table.

8. The red pen is used to grade papers.

9. He has a bad cold.

10. Principal Johnson suspended 10 students for misbehaving.

Section B.

Write 10 examples of a noun in the spaces below. Remember a noun can be either a person, place, or thing.

After you list 10 nouns circle either person, place, or thing to indicate what type of noun you listed.

1._____   person, place, thing

2._____   person, place, thing

3._____   person, place, thing

4._____   person, place, thing

5._____   person, place, thing

6._____   person, place, thing

7._____   person, place, thing

8._____   person, place, thing

9._____   person, place, thing

10._____   person, place, thing

Section C.

Write 6 complete sentences using a different noun in each sentence. Write 2 sentences with a noun that is a person, 2 sentences with a noun that is a place, and 2 sentences with a noun that is a thing.

1. _____

2._____

3._____

4._____

5._____

6._____

Verb? What is a verb?

(a) expresses an action or state of being (b) a pronoun (c) a preverb

If you selected answer (a) you are correct. A verb is a word that expresses action or a state of being. It is a word that tells about an occurrence or what happened in the sentence. Some examples of verbs are: run, jump, kick, pull, took, hop, waited, hit, kissed, was, were, is, am, be, been, being and are. Words that express action: run, jump, kick, pull, took, hop, waited, hit and kissed. Words that are a state of being: was, were, is, am, be, been, being and are.

In the activity below underline all the verbs in each sentence. After you underline the verbs label each with a letter V. {TYS LA 1ˢᵗ to 4ᵗʰ, 1 110.3(a)(1)(4), 2 110.4(b)(3)(e), 2 110.4(a), 3 110.5(a)(4), 4 110.6(a)(4)}

The first sentence is done for you.

1. Mrs. Walter <u>pushed </u>her grocery cart down the aisle.
                        V
2. The little girl ran to the playground.

3. The fairytale story is very funny.

4. George Bush became our president in the year 2000.

5. Will he find the watch in the desk?

6. My computer broke this morning.

7. May I have some coffee in the morning?

8. Please come to my office this evening.

9. The baseball team won the game in the last ending.

10. Your daughter rode her bicycle on the sidewalk.

Section B.

Write 10 examples of a verb in the spaces below. Remember a verb is a word that expresses action or is a state of being.

After you list 10 verbs circle either expresses action or state of being to indicate what type of verb you listed.

1._____   expresses action, state of being

2. _____   expresses action, state of being

3. _____   expresses action, state of being

4. _____   expresses action, state of being

5. _____   expresses action, state of being

6. _____   expresses action, state of being

7. _____   expresses action, state of being

8. _____   expresses action, state of being

9. _____   expresses action, state of being

10. _____   expresses action, state of being

Section C.

Write 6 sentences using a different verb in each sentence. Write 3 sentences using verbs that express action. Write 3 sentences using verbs that are a state of being.

1._____

2._____

3._____

4._____

5._____

6._____

Name_____Date_____

Adjectives? What is an adjective?

(a) a predicate (b) a person, place, or thing (c) a word describing a noun

If you selected answer (c) you are correct. An adjective is a word that describes a noun or pronoun. Adjectives tell what kind or how many? Examples of adjectives are: blue, yellow, green, black and other colors. Adjectives that describe are: little, tall, thin, thick, big, long. Adjectives that tell how many are 1 (one), 2 (two), 3 (three), 4 (four) etc.

Underline the adjectives in the sentences below and label the word with the abbreviation Adj. {TYS LA 1ˢᵗ to 4ᵗʰ, 1 110.3(a)(1)(4), 2 110.4(b)(3)(e), 2 110.4(a), 3 110.5(a)(4), 4 110.6(a)(4)}

1. The girl wore a beautiful dress.

2. The tall man walked in the door.

3. The child played with the blue ball.

4. Five students went to the science fair.

5. The powerful ape jumped on the man.

6. The striped horse is called a zebra.

7. The famous author wrote this book.

Section B:

Write 5 examples of Adjectives in the blanks below. Remember that Adjectives describe nouns and pronouns. They also tell what kind and how many? Also circle what type of Adjective you provided in the blank.

1._____ describe, what kind, how many?

2._____ describe, what kind, how many?

3._____describe, what kind, how many?

4._____describe, what kind, how many?

5. _____describe, what kind, how many?

Section C:

Write 6 sentences using adjectives to describe, tell what kind or how many?

1._____

2._____

3_____

4._____

5._____

6._____

Name_____ Date_____

Adverbs? What is an adverb?

An adverb is: A word that describes a verb. Adverbs tell how, when and where an action happens. Some adverbs end in –*ly*.

Directions: Underline the adverbs in the sentences below. Write the abbreviation **Adv** under the word. The first sentence is done for you. {TYS LA 1st to 4th, 1 110.3(a)(1)(4), 2 110.4(b)(3)(e), 2 110.4(a), 3 110.5(a)(4), 4 110.6(a)(4)}

Sentences:

1. The bus is moving <u>slowly</u> down the road.
                          Adv.

2. My mother will come to visit tomorrow.

3. My book is upstairs in the drawer.

4. The couple lived happily ever after.

5. The red motorcycle is moving fast.

6. My family will arrive later today.

7. First wash the dishes and then sweep the floor.

8. The boy ran slowly in the Olympic race.

Section B:

Write 8 examples of adverbs in the blanks below. Does your adverb tell how, when, where or does it end in –*ly*. Circle the correct meaning of your adverb.

1. _____how, when, where, -ly

2._____how, when, where, -ly

3._____ how, when, where, -ly

4._____ how, when, where, -ly

5._____ how, when, where, -ly

6._____ how, when, where, -ly

7._____ how, when, where, -ly

8._____ how, when, where, -ly

Section C:

Write 8 sentences using an adverb in each. Underline the adverb that you chose to use in each sentence.

1._____

2._____

3._____

4._____

5._____

6._____

7._____

8._____

Name_____ Date_____

What are Pronouns?

Proper Nouns ?

A pronoun takes the place of a noun. Examples of subject pronouns are: I, you, he, she, it, we, you, & they. Subject pronouns replace nouns that follow the verb *be.*   Examples of object pronouns are me, you, her, him, it, us, you, & them. Object pronouns replace nouns after *action verbs or after to, for, with, in or at.*

Proper Nouns name a particular person, place or thing. Proper nouns are also capitalized. Examples are: Mrs. Dobbs, Atlantic Ocean, Red Sea, Pecan Street, Africa, St. Luke Apartments.

Directions: Replace the Proper Nouns in each sentence below with a pronoun. Write a pronoun below the noun. The first sentence is done for you. {TYS LA 1st to 4th, 1 110.3(a)(1)(4), 2 110.4(b)(3)(e), 2 110.4(a), 3 110.5(a)(4), 4 110.6(a)(4)}

Sentences:

1. Rebecca wants a bicycle for a present.
   She

2. The White House has many rooms.

3. Jennifer is a good student.

4. The Lincoln Tigers won the game.

5. The Oprah Show will air tonight at 8:00 p.m.

6. Shirley and I went to the movies last weekend.

7. The hat belongs to Mrs. Lucy.

Section B:

Directions: Replace the Pronouns with Proper Nouns in the sentences below. The first sentence is done for you.

1. She is a good teacher.
   Mrs. Soto

2. They are members of the team.

3. He is the principal of this school.

4. We love to go to the fair.

5. He is a big dog.

The Young Scholar's Book Club

Name_____Date_____

Sentence Structure TEST

Definitions: Read each word below and circle the letter that has the correct definition of the word.

1. Noun

    a. something you describe   b. a person, place, or thing

    c. a word   d. a sentence part

2. Verb

    a. a word that expresses action   b. a pronoun that describes

    c. something that tells a story   d. an exciting word

3. Adjective

    a. a word preposition   b. a prediction

    c. a word that describes a noun   d. a future event

4. Pronoun

    a. a verb   b. a word that describes a noun

    c. a contraction   d. a word that takes the place of a noun

Section B:

Sentences: Underline the Noun, Verb, Adjective, and Pronoun

Label each one as: Noun= N, Adjective= A, Pronoun= P, Verb= V,

1. Lucy fell down on the red carpet.

2. She smiled at the big clown.

3. The thick book dropped on her head.

4. He flew a yellow kite.

5. The blue car raced down the street.

6. She kicked the ball to the nice girl.

7. The blue pen writes very smooth.

8. It is on the brown table.

Section C:

Nouns-   Write 6 examples of a noun
1.
2.
3.
4.
5.
6.

Adjectives- Write 6 examples of an adjective
1.
2.
3.
4.
5.
6.

Pronouns- Write 6 examples of a pronoun
1.
2.
3.
4.
5.
6.

Verbs-   Write 6 examples of a verb
1.
2.
3.
4.
5.
6.

The Young Scholar's Book Club

Name_____ Date_____

ABC ORDER

Directions: Put each word group in alphabetical order.
{TYS LA 1ˢᵗ to 4ᵗʰ, 1 110.3(b)(5)(e)}

1. eat   _____
2. budget   _____
3. silver   _____
4. alarm   _____
5. ebony   _____
6. park   _____
7. earth   _____
8. hero   _____
9. farm   _____
10. build   _____

1. child   _____
2. about   _____
3. lake   _____
4. pond   _____
5. ground   _____
6. age   _____
7. feather   _____
8. bank   _____
9. brick   _____
10. sea   _____

1. zoo   _____
2. watch   _____
3. sun   _____
4. sad   _____
5. cut   _____
6. salt   _____
7. sign   _____
8. under   _____
9. where   _____
10. coat   _____

1. ship   _____
2. flower   _____
3. win   _____
4. water   _____
5. cup   _____
6. phone   _____
7. card   _____
8. flag   _____
9. pipe   _____
10. down   _____

Name_____ Date_____

ABC ORDER QUIZ

Directions: Put each word in alphabetical order.
{TYS LA 1ˢᵗ to 4ᵗʰ, 1 110.3(b)(5)(e)}

1. mile _____
2. skirt _____
3. sign _____
4. wife _____
5. apple _____
6. animal _____
7. left _____
8. base _____
9. cow _____
10. even _____
11. right _____
12. evil _____
13. shirt _____
14. every _____
15. crab _____

The Young Scholar's Book Club

Name_____ Date_____

What is a Fact? What is an Opinion?

A fact is information that is true and can be proven.
An opinion is your thought or feeling about something.

Example: My dress is red. (This sentence states a fact)
         The dress is pretty (This sentence states an opinion)

Write (F) for Fact or (O) for Opinion in the blank after each
sentence. {TYS LA 1st to 4th, 3 110.5(a), 4 110.6(b)(2)(c)}

1. The teacher graduated from Dallas Baptist University._____

2. My car is red and black._____

3. The principal said football is the best sport. _____

4. The woman lives at 8765 West Lupiter in Vermont._____

5. Mrs. Gladiar says roses are better than tulips. _____

6. Mr. Gumpier is the best teacher in 5th grade. _____

7. Roller Elementary is located at 7890 Junio Lane. _____

8. Rose Perry is not a good doctor. _____

The Young Scholar's Book Club

Name_____ Date_____

FACT? Or OPINION?

Facts- are identified by true statements and statements that can be proven.

Opinions- are identified by feelings, thoughts, or beliefs. Opinions are not necessarily proven.

Directions: Look at the sentences below. Carefully read each sentence. Label each sentence as fact or opinion. Write your answer in the space provided. {TYS LA 1st to 4th, 3 110.5(a), 4 110.6(b)(2)(c)}

1. Mrs. Calvert works for Ford Motor Company._____

2. The computer on the last row works better. _____

3. The cake is blue and white. _____

4. The blocks are fun to play with._____

5. All children like arcade games._____

6. Mr. Zack graduated in 1975._____

7. The Dallas Cowboys won several championships. _____

8. Computers have monitors to view information._____

9. The dictionary is for looking up words and their meaning._____

Section II: 1st to 4th Grade

Reading

The Young Scholar's Book Club

Name_____ Date_____

Title: The Lady in the Box
Author: Ann McGovern
{TYS Reading 1st to 4th, 1 110.3(b)(9)(b), 2 110.4(b)(6)(b), 3 110.5(b)(6)(b), 4 110.6(b)(7)(b)}

Definitions:
1. deli_____
2. basement_____
3. freezing_____
4. homeless_____
5. shelter_____
6. charity_____
7. soup kitchen_____
8. two flights of stairs_____
9. hungry_____

Questions:
1. Describe the setting of the story?

_____

2. What time of year does this story take place?

_____

3. What evidence in the pictures show the time of year?

_____

4. Name all the characters in the story.

_____

5. _____ and _____
   see a lady who is _____ and
   _____.
6. What is the homeless lady's name?_____
7. The children help the lady by giving her
   _____ and_____.
8. Where does the lady live?_____
9. Why does the lady move from in front of the Circle
   Deli?_____
10. Who do the children tell about the
    lady?_____.
11. The children and their mother volunteer at
    the_____ to help homeless people.
12. What does Ben want the homeless lady to have one
    day?_____
13. What does he give the homeless lady at the end of
    the story?_____

Bonus Questions:
1. Who is the publisher of this book?

_____

2. Who is the illustrator of this book?

_____

3. Is this book fiction or non-fiction?

_____

The Young Scholar's Book Club

Name_____ Date_____

Title: Tonio's Cat
Author: Mary Calhoun
{TYS Reading 1st to 4th, 1 110.3(b)(9)(b), 2 110.4(b)(6)(b), 3 110.5(b)(6)(b), 4 110.6(b)(7)(b)}

Definitions:
1. Mexico-_____

2. California- _____

3. Cazador-_____

4. gato-_____

5. apartments-_____

6. cage-_____

7. angry-_____

Questions
1. List all of the characters in the story

2. What country is Tonio from?

3. What was the name of Tonio's first pet?

4. What animal followed Tonio around?

5. Did Tonio like this animal at first?

6. What did Tonio name this animal?

7. What did Tonio's mother tell him about keeping this animal?

8. How did Tonio later feel about this animal?

9. What did Tonio do to protect and care for this animal?

Name_____ Date_____

Title: The Gold Cadillac
Author: Mildred D. Taylor
{TYS Reading 1ˢᵗ to 4ᵗʰ, 1 110.3(b)(9)(b), 2 110.4(b)(6)(b), 3 110.5(b)(6)(b), 4 110.6(b)(7)(b)}

Definitions:
1. Cadillac-_____

2. Mother Dear-_____

3. grinned-_____

4. second floor duplex-_____

5. unison-_____

6. lynch-_____

7. uppity-_____

Questions:
1. List all the characters in the "The Gold Cadillac"

2. What did the father in the story bring home for the family to see?

3. What did Lois and Wilma do when they saw their father's surprise?

4. Who was not excited about the surprise?

5. Where did the father decide to drive the family?

6. Who advised the father against his decision and why?

7. What happened when the family went out of town?

8. Why do you think this incident happened?

Section II: 1st to 4th Grade

Mathematics

Name_____ Date_____

2 Digit Addition & Subtraction

Watch the signs to Add or Subtract.
{TYS Math 1ˢᵗ to 4ᵗʰ, 2 111.14(b)(3)(a), 3 111.15(b)(3)(b), 4 111.16(b)(3)(a)}

1. 89   2. 90   3. 70   4. 29
   +12   +25   -15   -14

5. 11   6. 45   7. 67   8. 99
   +10   -16   -12   +45

9. 89   10. 59   11. 40   12. 39
   -41   - 39   +29   + 39

Name_____ Date_____

Multiplication & Division

{TYS Math 1ˢᵗ to 4ᵗʰ, 3 111.15(b)(4), 4 111.16(b)(4)(d)(e)}

(1)   25
    x   3

(2)   7
    x   8

(3)   10
    x 12

(4)   3
    x   8

(5)   9
    x 6

(6)   1
    x 9

(7)   24
    x   2

(8)   18
    x   3

(9)   16
    x   2

(10)   2
     x   9

Multiplication & Division continued...

(11) $\dfrac{16}{8}$ (12) $\dfrac{28}{7}$ (13) $\dfrac{50}{10}$ (14) $\dfrac{36}{6}$

(15) $\dfrac{30}{15}$ (16) $\dfrac{8}{4}$ (17) $\dfrac{49}{7}$ (18) $\dfrac{100}{50}$

(19) $\dfrac{35}{7}$ (20) $\dfrac{81}{9}$

Name_____Date_____

Improper & Mixed Fractions

Solve each fraction below to its simplest form. {TYS Math 1st to 4th, 1
111.13(b)(2), 3 111.15(b)(2), 4 111.16(b)(2)}

1. $\dfrac{1}{2}$ =

2. $\dfrac{2}{10}$ =

3. $1\dfrac{5}{25}$ =

4. $3\dfrac{25}{50}$ =

5. $4\dfrac{7}{42}$ =

6. $\dfrac{15}{30} =$

7. $\dfrac{81}{9} =$

8. $7\dfrac{8}{10} =$

9. $6\dfrac{6}{36} =$

10. $\dfrac{8}{32} =$

The Young Scholar's Book Club

Name_____Date_____

Area and Perimeter

Mathematic Formulas:
Area: L x W = A
Length x Width = A
Perimeter: (2 x L) + (2 x H) = P
2(Length) + 2(Height) = P

Area is the total space within a given border.

Perimeter is the border of a given area.

Find the area in each problem below. Show your work.
{TYS Math 1st to 4th, 3 111.15(b)(11), 4 111.16(b)(12)}

(1)

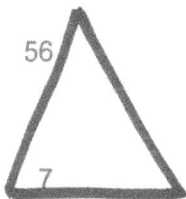

(2)

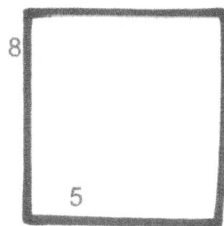

(3)

(4)

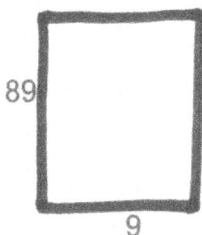

(5)

(6)

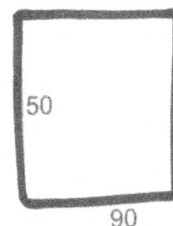

Area and Perimeter continued.......

Find the perimeter of each problem below. Show your work.

(7)

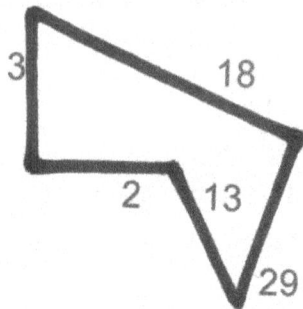

(8)

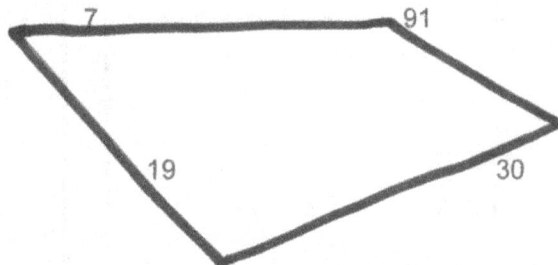

(9)

(10)

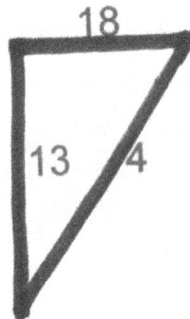

(11)

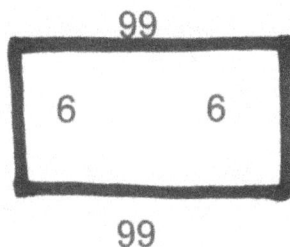

(12)

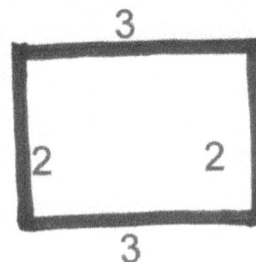

Section II: 1st to 4th Grade

Social Studies

The Young Scholar's Book Club

Name_____ Date_____

The Gettysburg Address

Materials needed for this lesson:

Book: *The Gettysburg Address* by Kenneth Richards

You can obtain this book by purchasing it from your local bookstore or check it out at your local library. You can also use the internet for this activity.

Directions: Read the book **The Gettysburg Address** by Kenneth Richards and answer the questions below. {TYS Social Studies 1ˢᵗ to 4ᵗʰ, 1 113.3(a)(4), 1 113.3(b)(1)(a), 1 113.3(b)(10)(11), 2 113.4(a)(4), 3 113.5(a)(4), 4 113.6(a)(4)}

1. Write a short definition of the

   Gettysburg Address?_____

   _____

   _____

 2. What was the major problem between the Northern States and Southern States during the 1850's?_____

   _____

3. In 1860, who was elected president of the United States?_____

 4. Was this president democrat or republican?

   _____

   _____

5. What was this president's position on the problem the Northern and Southern States had in 1860?

_____

_____

_____

6. After a president was elected in 1860 what did some do states before he was inaugurated?

_____

_____

_____

7. Which states took part in the event?_____

_____

_____

8. What was the Civil War and what caused it?

_____

_____

_____

9. When did the Civil War end?_____

_____

_____

Name_____Date_____

What is a Democracy?

Materials needed for this lesson: Any history book, encyclopedia or internet.

Directions: Read information about Democracy from an encyclopedia or history book and answer the questions below. {TYS Social Studies 1st to 4th, 1 113.3(a)(4), 1 113.3(b)(1)(a), 1 113.3(b)(10)(11), 2 113.4(a)(4), 3 113.5(a)(4), 4 113.6(a)(4)}

Questions:

1. Write a short definition about Democracy?

2. Who rules in a Democracy?

3. Name two other forms of government used in other countries?

4. What form of government does the United States have?

5. What form of government does Russia and Africa have?

6. How does democracy work?

7. What name is given where no laws or government exists?

Name_____Date_____

United States Government: 3 Branches

What are they? Executive, Legislative, & Judicial

Materials and Books: American Government and Politics Today by Steffen W. Schmidt or any government or history book, encyclopedia or internet.

The United States has a government that operates with three branches. The three branches of government are Executive, Legislative, and Judicial. Each branch has a different function and all depend on each other. The Executive branch involves the president and his roles, the Legislative branch involves congress and their roles, and the Judicial branch involves the Supreme Court and their roles. {TYS Social Studies 1st to 4th, 1 113.3(a)(4), 1 113.3(b)(1)(a), 1 113.3(b)(10)(11), 2 113.4(a)(4), 3 113.5(a)(4), 4 113.6(a)(4)}

Questions:

1. Give 5 roles that the president of the United States has within the Executive branch.

2. The Legislative branch is made up of two bodies. What are they?

3. Explain the process of how an idea becomes law.

4. Explain the roles of Congress.

5. Explain the roles of the Supreme Court.

6. What does impeach mean?

7. Why would a president be impeached?

Section II: 1st to 4th Grade

Science

The Young Scholar's Book Club

Name_____Date_____

Our Solar System: 9 Planets

Materials and Books: The Big Book of Space Discovery by Schmidt-Cannon International. You can also use any science book, encyclopedia or internet.

Our Solar System is made of 9 planets. These planets are Earth, Mercury, Venus, Mars, Saturn, Jupiter, Pluto, Neptune, and Uranus. Astronomy is the study of the planets and objects beyond the earth. Those who study the planets and stars are called astronomers. They use the telescope to help with their research. **{TYS Science 1st to 4th, 1 112.3(a)(4)(5), 2 112.4(a)(4)(5), 3 112.5(b)(11)(c), 4 112.6(a)(5)(6)}**

Questions:

1. What planet do we live on?

2. Name the smallest planet in the universe.

3. Which two planets have a special ring around them?

4. How many days does it take the planet earth to rotate around the sun? How many days does it take Jupiter?

5. Which planet is the furthest from the sun? Which Planet is the closest to the sun?

6. Who was the first U.S. astronaut to travel in space? Who was the first woman?

7. Who were the first astronauts to land on the moon? What day and year?

8. Put the planets in order: Starting with the one
   closest to the sun to the one furthest from the sun.

Name_____ Date_____

Using the Microscope

Materials and Books: You can use any science book, encyclopedia or the internet. It is also helpful to have a microscope.

The microscope is an optical instrument having a magnifying lens for inspecting objects that are too small to be seen by the naked eye. **(The Random House College Dictionary)**
{TYS Science 1st to 4th, 3 112.5(b)(4)(a)(b)}

Questions:

1. List 9 parts of the Microscope:

2. Circle the object that can only be seen through a microscope.

    a. orange   b. bacteria   c. truck   d. butterfly

3. What does the prefix *micro* mean?

4. List 5 things that you can only see through a microscope.

5. Write a short paragraph of how to use a microscope.

The Young Scholar's Book Club

Name _____ Date_____

Electricity? Who? When? Where? Why?

Materials & Books: You can use an encyclopedia, dictionary, any science book or the internet.

Have you ever wondered where electricity comes from and why it is an important resource in our society? Electricity is a powerful force in our universe. It has always existed from the beginning of time. It took man to discover and find ways to utilize this mysterious resource. In this activity you will investigate and answer the question that was presented at the beginning of this lesson. Where does electricity come from? You will also do further investigation to find out who discovered electricity and what are some uses for it? *{TYS Science 1st to 4th grade, 1 112.3 a(1)(2) b(3)(c) b(2)(b)(d)(e), 2 112.4 a(5) b(2)(b)(f) 3(c), 3 112.5 a(5) b(11)(a) b(11)(c) 4 112.6 a(1)(2) b(4)(a) b(5)(a)}*

Read the questions carefully and fill in the blanks with the correct answer below.

1. What is the definition of electricity?_____

_____

2. Who is given credit in history for discovering electricity?_____

_____

3. How & why was electricity discovered?_____

_____

4. What is a lightening bolt?_____

_____

_____

5. Who was the first scientist to start experimenting with electricity?

_____

6. What was the name of the book he wrote to report his findings about electricity?

_____

7. Which century did scientists finally begin to make progress in understanding electricity?

_____

8. What did scientists store electricity in to contain and study it?

_____

9. Name 3 other ways electricity is contained and stored for use?

_____

10. What do we use electricity for today?_____

_____

11. How did people survive in the past without electricity? _____

_____

The Young Scholar's Book Club

Name_____Date_____

The Scientific Method

Materials and Books: Science books, encyclopedia or internet
Use a separate sheet of paper. Search the internet for 1st to 4ᵗʰ grade science projects.

The Scientific Method uses ordered steps to investigate a science experiment. The steps are: 1. State the question or problem 2. Research the question or problem 3. Form a Hypothesis
4. Experiment 5. Observe and take notes 6. Analyze the data
7. Draw a conclusion *{TYS Science 1ˢᵗ to 4ᵗʰ grade, 1 112.3 a(1)(2) b(3)(c) b(2)(b)(d)(e), 2 112.4 a(5) b(2)(b)(f) 3(c), 3 112.5 a(5) b(11)(a) b(11)(c) 4 112.6 a(1)(2) b(4)(a) b(5)(a)}*

Science Project:

1. State your question or problem for your science project. What do you want to find out?

2. Research your question or problem. You can go to the library to check out books on your question or problem. Search the internet, encyclopedias, science books or interview professionals on your subject.

3. After you do your research write a Hypothesis. A Hypothesis is an educated guess. What do you think will be the outcome of your problem or question?

Copyright © 2012 The Young Scholar's Workbook: Book I Vol. I www.tysbookclub.com 181

4. It is now time to test your Hypothesis. Do an experiment. Gather the materials you need to do your experiment. Write a list of everything you used in the experiment. Write down the steps you followed to perform your experiment.

5. During the experiment make sure you write down what happens. What did you see, smell, hear, or observe?

6. Now take your notes and analyze what you wrote in your notes. Analyze what happened in the experiment. Analyze means to look at every detail, write down the causes and effects of the details and write the results.

7. Draw a Conclusion. Write down your result or answer for your problem or question. What was the final result? Did you predict the correct answer for your Hypothesis?

Section II: 1st to 4th Grade

Writing

Name_____Date_____

The Writing Process—Prewriting—Write a First Draft—Revise—Proofread—Publish

Write a personal narrative about a vacation that you enjoyed. The story should be 1 page long.
{TYS Writing 1st to 4th, 1 110.3(b)(k), 2 110.4(b)(11)(b), 3 110.5(a)(4), 4 110.6(a)(4)}

1. The writing process starts with prewriting. Prewriting includes choosing a good topic.   Write out the details you want to include in your paper.
   You can also use an outline to help you organize your story.
2. Next, use your outline to write your first draft. Tell your story in the order it happened.
3. When your first draft is finished revise it. Check for spelling mistakes, grammar, sentence structure and what you may want to take out or add to your story.
4. Proofread your story and check again for errors.
5. Publish the final draft of your story and share it with others.

The Young Scholar's Book Club

Name_____ Date_____

Writing Prompts.......................

The Writing Process—Prewriting—Write a First Draft—
Revise—Proofread—Publish

1. The writing process starts with prewriting. Prewriting includes choosing a good topic. Write out the details you want to include in your paper. You can also use an outline to help you organize your story.
2. Next, use your outline to write your first draft. Tell your story in the order it happened.
3. When your first draft is finished revise it. Check for spelling mistakes, grammar, sentence structure and what you may want to take out or add to your story.
4. Proofread your story and check again for errors.
5. Publish the final draft of your story and share it with others.

{TYS Writing 1st to 4th, 1 110.3(b)(k), 2 110.4(b)(11)(b), 3 110.5(a)(4), 4 110.6(a)(4)}

Use the same format above when you create your own stories from the writing prompts below. Use a separate sheet of paper to write about……..

1. A time you were scared.
2. A special time you spent with your grandparents.
3. Your favorite family pet.
4. 3 things you love about your favorite T.V. show.
5. Your future career.
6. Your favorite book.
7. The famous person you admire.
8. What you admire most in your parents.
9. Your favorite hobby.

Section II: 1st to 4th Grade

Answer Key

1ˢᵗ to 4ᵗʰ Grade Language Arts Key

The Young Scholar's Book Club

Name _____ Date _____

Noun? What is a noun?

(a.) an action word (b.) a person, place, or thing (c.) a descriptive word

If you chose answer (b) you are correct. A noun is a person, place, or thing. Examples of some nouns are: Mr. Samson, The Grand Canyon, Lucy, toys. Mr. Samson is a person, The Grand Canyon is a place, Lucy is a person, and toys are things.

In the activity below underline all the nouns in each sentence. After you underline the nouns label each with a letter N. (TYS LA 1ˢᵗ to 4ᵗʰ, 1 110.3(a)(1)(4), 2 110.4(b)(3)(e), 3 110.4(a), 3 110.5(a)(4), 4 110.6(a)(4))

The first sentence is done for you

1. The woman went to the store to buy a coat.
2. Yellow Stone Park is a great place to visit.
3. The dog ran across the street.
4. The silver watch is pretty.
5. Mother Goose is a fairytale character.
6. The black truck raced down the freeway.
7. My blue folder is on the table.
8. The red pen is used to grade papers.
9. He has a bad cold.
10. Principal Johnson suspended 10 students for misbehaving.

The Young Scholar's Workbook: Book 1, Vol. 1 www.tysbookclub.com

---

Write 10 examples of a noun in the spaces below. Remember a noun can be either a person, place, or thing

After you list 10 nouns circle either person, place, or thing to indicate what type of noun you listed

1. Park — person, (place), thing
2. Woman — (person), place, thing
3. man — (person), place, thing
4. boy — (person), place, thing
5. girl — (person), place, thing
6. book — person, place, (thing)
7. TV — person, place, (thing)
8. Car — person, place, (thing)
9. Mrs. Jones — (person), place, thing
10. Disney land — person, (place), thing

Answers Will Vary

Write 6 complete sentences using a different noun in each sentence. Write 2 sentences with a noun that is a person, 2 sentences with a noun that is a place, and 2 sentences with a noun that is a thing.

1. Keisha went to school.
2. Principal Jones gave the order.
3. Disney land is my vacation spot.
4. Houston is my home town.
5. My T.V. is small.
6. His car is pink.

answers will vary

The Young Scholar's Book Club

Name _____ Date _____

Verb? What is a verb?

(a) expresses an action or state of being (b) a pronoun (c) a proverb

If you selected answer (a) you are correct. A verb is a word that expresses action or a state of being. It is a word that tells about an occurrence or what happened in the sentence. Some examples of verbs are: run, jump, kick, pull, took, hop, wanted, fan, kissed, was, were, is, am, be, been, being, are. Words that express action: run, jump, kick, pull, took, hop, wanted, hit, and kissed. Words that are a state of being: was, were, is, am, be, been, being, and are

In the activity below underline all the verbs in each sentence. After you underline the verbs label each with a letter V. (TYS LA 1ˢᵗ to 4ᵗʰ, 1 110.3(a)(1)(4), 2 110.4(b)(3)(e), 3 110.4(a), 3 110.5(a)(4), 4 110.6(a)(4))

The first sentence is done for you

1. Mrs. Walter pushed her grocery cart down the aisle.
2. The little girl ran to the playground.
3. The fairy tale story is very funny.
4. George Bush became our president in the year 2000.
5. Will he find the watch in the desk?
6. My computer broke this morning.
7. May I have some coffee in the morning?
8. Please come to my office this evening.
9. The baseball team won the game in the last inning.
10. Your daughter rode her bicycle on the sidewalk.

The Young Scholar's Workbook: Book 1, Vol. 1 www.tysbookclub.com

---

Write 10 examples of a verb in the spaces below. Remember a verb is a word that expresses action or is a state of being.

After you list 10 verbs circle either expresses action or state of being to indicate what type of verbs you listed

1. ran — (expresses action), state of being
2. wrote — (expresses action), state of being
3. scream — (expresses action), state of being
4. rode — (expresses action), state of being
5. look — (expresses action), state of being
6. buy — (expresses action), state of being
7. is — expresses action, (state of being)
8. told — (expresses action), state of being
9. was — expresses action, (state of being)
10. are — expresses action, (state of being)

answers will vary

Write 6 sentence using a different verb in each sentence. Write 3 sentences using verbs that express action. Write 3 sentences using verbs that are a state of being.

1. He rode his bike home.
2. She bought new shoes.
3. Ms. Jenn told the truth.
4. Crystal is a girl.
5. Bob was at school.
6. Richard is silly.

Answers will vary

The Young Scholar's Book Club

Name _____ Date _____

Adjectives? What is an adjective?

(a) a predicate (b) a person, place, or thing (c) a word describing a noun

If you selected answer (c) you are correct. An adjective is a word that describes a noun or pronoun. Adjectives tell what kind or how many? Examples of adjectives are: blue, yellow, green, black and other colors. Adjectives that describe are: little, tall, thin, thick, big, long. Adjectives that tell how many are: 1 (one), 2 (two), 3 (three), 4 (four) etc.

Underline the adjectives in the sentences below and label the word with the abbreviation Adj. (TYS LA 1ˢᵗ to 4ᵗʰ, 1 110.3(a)(1)(4), 2 110.4(b)(3)(e), 3 110.4(a), 3 110.5(a)(4), 4 110.6(a)(4))

1. The girl wore a beautiful dress.
   Adj
2. The tall man walked in the door.
   Adj
3. The child played with the blue ball.
   Adj
4. Five students went to the science fair.
   Adj

The Young Scholar's Workbook: Book 1, Vol. 1 www.tysbookclub.com

---

5. The powerful ape jumped on the man.
   Adj
6. The striped horse is called a zebra.
   Adj
7. The famous author wrote this book
   Adj

Write 5 examples of Adjectives in the blanks below. Remember that Adjectives describe nouns and pronouns. They also tell what kind and how many? Also circle what type of Adjective you provided in the blank.

1. 5 horses — describe, what kind, (how many?)
2. blue purse — describe, (what kind) how many?
3. Small child — (describe) what kind, how many?
4. tall man — (describe) what kind, how many?
5. Six horses — describe, what kind, (how many?)

The Young Scholar's Workbook: Book 1, Vol. 1 www.tysbookclub.com

---

Write 6 sentences using adjectives to describe, tell what kind or how many?

1. My blue dress is pretty.
2. My mother has 5 dogs.
3. The thin girl climbed the tree.
4. The fat cat ran to him.
5. Seven men voted for her.
6. The red car belongs to Cindy.

example sentences.

188

Panel 1 (page 135):

Name_____ Date_____

Adverbs? What is an adverb?

An adverb is: A word that describes a verb. Adverbs tell how, when and where an action happens. Some adverbs end in –ly.

Directions: Underline the adverbs in the sentences below. Write the abbreviation *Adv* under the word. The first sentence is done for you. (TYS LA 1st to 4th, 1 110.3(a)(1)(A), 2 110.4(b)(3)(A), 3 110.5(a)(3), 4 110.6(a)(4))

Sentences:

1. The bus is moving <u>slowly</u> down the road.
   Adv.

2. My mother will come to visit <u>tomorrow</u>.
   Adv.

3. My book is <u>upstairs</u> in the drawer.
   Adv.

4. The couple lived <u>happily</u> ever after.
   Adv.

Panel 2 (page 136):

5. The red motorcycle is moving <u>fast</u>.
   Adv.

6. My family will arrive <u>later today</u>.
   Adv.

7. <u>First</u> wash the dishes and then sweep the floor.
   Adv.   **Adv.**

8. The boy ran <u>slowly</u> in the Olympic race.
   Adv.

Section B:

Write 8 examples of adverbs in the blanks below. Does your adverb tell how, when, where or does it end in –ly. Circle the correct meaning of your adverb.

1. Swiftly   how, when, where, (-ly)
2. last   how, (when,) where, -ly
3. yesterday   how, (when,) where, -ly
4. inside   how, when, (where,) -ly

Panel 3 (page 137):

5. often   how, (when,) where, -ly
6. secretly   (how,) when, where, (-ly)
7. downtown   how, when, (where,) -ly
8. next   how, (when,) where, -ly

Section C:

Write 8 sentences using an adverb in each. Underline the adverb that you chose to use in each sentence.   Answers Vary

1. He worked <u>quickly</u>.
2. Robin is <u>next</u> in line.
3. Grandma shopped <u>inside the mall</u>.
4. The bell rang <u>loudly</u>.

Panel 4 (page 138):

5. Peter <u>secretly</u> gave her a note.
6. Barbara <u>easily</u> passed her test.
7. <u>Yesterday</u> was his birthday.
8. <u>First</u> he went home then he went to the party.

Panel 5:

Name_____ Date_____

What are Pronouns?
Proper Nouns?

A pronoun takes the place of a noun. Examples of subject pronouns are: I, you, he, she, it, we, you, & they. Subject pronouns replace nouns that follow the verb *be*. Examples of object pronouns are me, you, her, him, it, us, you, & them. Object pronouns replace nouns after *action verbs or after to, for, with, in or at*.

Proper Nouns name a particular person, place or thing. Proper nouns are also capitalized. Examples are: Mrs. Dobbs, Atlantic Ocean, Red Sea, Pecan Street, Africa, St. Luke Apartments.

Directions: Replace the Proper Nouns in each sentence below with a pronoun. Write a pronoun below the noun. The first sentence is done for you. (TYS LA 1st to 4th, 1 110.3(a)(1)(A), 2 110.4(b)(3), 3 110.5(a)(3), 4 110.6(a)(4))

Sentences:

1. Rebecca wants a bicycle for a present.
   She

Panel 6:

2. The White House has many rooms.
   it

3. Jennifer is a good student.
   She

4. The Lincoln Tigers won the game.
   They

5. The Oprah Show will air tonight at 8:00 p.m.
   it

6. Shirley and I went to the movies last weekend.
   we

7. The hat belongs to Mrs. Lucy.
   It   her

Panel 7:

Section B:

Directions: Replace the Pronouns with Proper Nouns in the sentences below. The first sentence is done for you.

1. She is a good teacher.
   Mrs. Soto

2. They are members of the team.
   Jim and Bob

3. He is the principal of this school.
   Sam Washington

4. We love to go to the fair.
   Cindy and Jill

5. He is a big dog.
   James

Panel 8 (page 142):

Name_____ Date_____

Sentence Structure TEST

Definitions: Read each word below and circle the letter that has the correct definition of the word.

1. Noun
   a. something you describe   (b.) a person, place, or thing
   c. a word   d. a sentence part

2. Verb
   (a.) a word that expresses action   b. a pronoun that describes
   c. something that tells a story   d. an exciting word

3. Adjective
   a. a word preposition   b. a prediction
   (c.) a word that describes a noun   d. a future event

4. Pronoun
   a. a word   b. a word that describes a noun
   c. a contraction   (d.) a word that takes the place of a noun

---

Panel 9 (page 143):

Section B:

Sentences: Underline the Noun, Verb, Adjective, and Pronoun.

Label each one as: Noun= N, Adjective= A, Pronoun= P, Verb= V.

1. <u>Lucy</u> <u>fell</u> down on the <u>red</u> <u>carpet</u>.
   N   V   A   N

2. <u>She</u> <u>smiled</u> at the <u>big</u> <u>clown</u>.
   P   V   A   N

3. The <u>thick</u> <u>book</u> <u>dropped</u> on her <u>head</u>.
        A   N   V   N

4. <u>He</u> <u>flew</u> a <u>yellow</u> <u>kite</u>.
   P   V   A   N

5. The <u>blue</u> <u>car</u> <u>raced</u> down the <u>street</u>.
        A   N   V   N

6. <u>She</u> <u>kicked</u> the <u>ball</u> to the <u>nice</u> <u>girl</u>.
   P   V   N   A   N

7. The <u>blue</u> <u>pen</u> <u>writes</u> very smooth.
        A   N   V

8. <u>It</u> <u>is</u> on the <u>brown</u> <u>table</u>.
   P   V   A   N

Panel 1 (page 144)

Section C.

Nouns- Write 6 examples of a noun
1. basket
2. ball
3. dress
4. shoes
5. house
6. fan

ANSWERS
WILL
VARY

Adjectives- Write 6 examples of an adjective
1. blue
2. four
3. big
4. tall
5. little
6. Pretty

Pronouns- Write 6 examples of a pronoun
1. he
2. she
3. I
4. they
5. Them
6. we

Verbs- Write 6 examples of a verb
1. ran
2. break
3. bring
4. work
5. see
6. Speak

144

Panel 2 (page 145)

Name_____ Date_____

ABC ORDER

Directions: Put each word group in alphabetical order.
[TYS LA 1st to 4th, 1 110.3(b)(5)(e)]

1. eat — alarm
2. budget — budget
3. silver — build
4. alarm — earth
5. ebony — eat
6. park — ebony
7. earth — farm
8. hero — hero
9. farm — Park
10. build — Silver

1. child — about
2. about — age
3. lake — bank
4. pond — build → brick
5. ground — Child
6. age — feather
7. feather — ground
8. bank — lake
9. brick — pond
10. build → sea

1. zoo — Coat
2. watch — Cut
3. sun — Sad
4. sad — Salt
5. salt — Sign
6. sign — Sun
7. under — under
8. where — Watch
9. coat — Where
10. — zoo

1. ship — Card
2. flower — Cup
3. win — down
4. water — flag
5. cup — flower
6. phone — Phone
7. flag — Pipe
8. word — Ship
9. pipe — Water
10. down — Win

Panel 3 (page 146)

Name_____ Date_____

ABC ORDER QUIZ

Directions: Put each word in alphabetical order.
[TYS LA 1st to 4th, 1 110.3(b)(5)(e)]

1. mile — animal
2. skirt — apple
3. sign — base
4. wife — cow
5. apple — crab
6. animal — even
7. left — every
8. base — evil
9. cow — left
10. even — mile
11. right — right
12. evil — Shirt
13. shirt — Sign
14. every — Skirt
15. crab — Wife

146

Panel 4

Name_____ Date_____

What is a Fact? What is an Opinion?

A fact is information that is true and can be proven.
An opinion is your thought or feeling about something

Example: My dress is red. (This sentence states a fact)
The dress is pretty. (This sentence states an opinion)

Write (F) for Fact or (O) for Opinion in the blank after each sentence. [TYS LA 1st to 4th, 3 110.8(a), 4 110.6(b)(2)(e)]

1. The teacher graduated from Dallas Baptist University. **F**

2. My car is red and black. **F**

3. The principal said football is the best sport. **O**

4. The woman lives at 8765 West Jupiter in Vermont. **F**

5. Mrs. Gladiar says roses are better than tulips. **O**

6. Mr. Gumpier is the best teacher in 5th grade. **O**

7. Roller Elementary is located at 7890 Junio Lane. **F**

8. Rose Perry is not a good doctor. **O**

9. This computer has Windows 2000 installed in it. **F**

10. The NAACP is an exemplary organization. **O**

Panel 5

Name_____ Date_____

FACT? Or OPINION?

Facts- are identified by true statements and statements that can be proven.

Opinions- are identified by feelings, thoughts, or beliefs. Opinions are not necessarily proven.

Directions: Look at the sentences below. Carefully read each sentence. Label each sentence as fact or opinion. Write your answer in the space provided. [TYS LA 1st to 4th, 3 110.8(a), 4 110.6(b)(2)(e)]

1. Mrs. Calvert works for Ford Motor Company. **F**

2. The computer on the last row works better. **O**

3. The cake is blue and white. **F**

4. The blocks are fun to play with. **O**

5. All children like arcade games. **O**

6. Mr. Zack graduated in 1975. **F**

7. The Dallas Cowboys won several championships. **F**

8. Computers have monitors to view information. **F**

9. The dictionary is for looking up words and their meaning. **F**

10. Mrs. Rosa is the 4th grade science teacher at Zane Middle School. **F**

Panel 6 (page 150)

Name_____ Date_____

Title: The Lady in the Box
Author: Ann McGovern
[TYS Reading 1st to 4th, 1 110.3(b)(9)(b), 2 110.4(b)(6)(b), 3 110.5(b)(6)(b), 4 110.6(b)(7)(b)]

Definitions:
1. deli Place food is served.
2. basement is partly below the ground.
3. freezing liquid to ice when temp. changes.
4. homeless People without place to live.
5. shelter place to live, Protects you from outside.
6. charity free food, Shelter + Clothing.
7. soup kitchen Place to feed the needy.
8. two flights of stairs Series of Steps to next level.
9. hungry a strong need for food.

Questions:
1. Describe the setting of the story?
Winter, Snow, coats, hats, scarfs, Christmas.
2. What time of year does this story take place?
Winter at Christmas time.
3. What evidence in the pictures show the time of year?
Snow, Christmas lights, Coats.
4. Name all the characters in the story.
Lizzie Ben Moma Dorrie Circle Deli owner.

150

Panel 7 (page 151)

5. Lizzie and Ben see a lady who is hungry and homeless.
6. What is the homeless lady's name? Dorrie
7. The children help the lady by giving her Crackers and Peanut Butter.
8. Where does the lady live? in a box by circle Deli.
9. Why does the lady move from in front of the Circle Deli? Owner sent her away.
10. Who do the children tell about the lady? Their Moma.
11. The children and their mother volunteer at the Soup Kitchen to help homeless people.
12. What does Ben want the homeless lady to have one day? a job and place of her own.
13. What does he give the homeless lady at the end of the story? 4 leaf Clover luck Key ring.

Bonus Questions:
1. Who is the publisher of this book? Turtle Books
2. Who is the illustrator of this book? Marni Backer
3. Is this book fiction or non-fiction? fiction

Panel 8 (page 152)

Name_____ Date_____

Title: Tonio's Cat
Author: Mary Calhoun
[TYS Reading 1st to 4th, 1 110.3(b)(9)(b), 2 110.4(b)(6)(b), 3 110.5(b)(6)(b), 4 110.6(b)(7)(b)]

Definitions:
1. Mexico- Republic Country in S. North America.
2. California- US State on Pacific Coast.
3. Cazador- Tonio's dog in mexico.
4. gato- means cat in Spanish.
5. apartments- many rooms in one building.
6. cage- dwelling place for animals.
7. angry- show strong resentment.

Questions
1. List all of the characters in the story
Toni, Cazador, gato, mamá, Old lady Josefina Maria, Papá, Guadalupe, José Guillermo.
2. What country is Tonio from? Mexico

152

Panel 9 (page 153)

3. What was the name of Tonio's first pet?
Cazador
4. What animal followed Tonio around?
a cat, a gato
5. Did Tonio like this animal at first?
no because he wanted a dog.
6. What did Tonio name this animal?
gato
7. What did Tonio's mother tell him about keeping this animal? No pets allowed where he lived.
8. How did Tonio later feel about this animal?
He liked the cat and began to take care of it.
9. What did Tonio do to protect and care for this animal? He put the cat in a cage and fed it.

190

1st to 4th Grade Reading & Mathematics Key

Name_____ Date_____

Title: The Gold Cadillac
Author: Mildred D. Taylor

Definitions:
1. Cadillac- luxury automobile.
2. Mother Dear- Nickname for Lois + Wilma's mom
3. grinned- wide smile showing teeth
4. second floor duplex- twin units under 1 building.
5. unison- in agreement
6. lynch- to hang a person to cause death. It is illegal.
7. uppity- arrogant or snobbish

Questions:
1. List all the characters in the "The Gold Cadillac"
Wilbert, Dee, Lois, Wilma, Pondexter, Police Leroy, Courtland, aunts, uncles, Halton

2. What did the father in the story bring home for the family to see? Cadillac Car

3. What did Lois and Wilma do when they saw their father's surprise? They asked "Is it ours daddy?"

4. Who was not excited about the surprise? Mother Dear, Dee

5. Where did the father decide to drive the family? Mississippi to see his parents.

6. Who advised the father against his decision and why? Pondexter. It was a time of racism and discrimination against blacks.

7. What happened when the family went out of town? Police stopped Wilbert and searched him. Police thought Wilbert stole car.

8. Why do you think this incident happened? In 1950's there was racism, prejudice discrimination and mistreatment of blacks because of skin color.

Name_____ Date_____

2 Digit Addition & Subtraction

Watch the signs to Add or Subtract

1. 89 +12 = 101	2. 90 +25 = 115	3. 70 -15 = 55	4. 29 -14 = 15
5. 11 +10 = 21	6. 45 -16 = 29	7. 67 -12 = 55	8. 99 +45 = 144
9. 89 -41 = 48	10. 59 -39 = 20	11. 40 +29 = 69	12. 39 +39 = 78

Name_____ Date_____

Multiplication & Division

(1) 25 x 3 = 75	(2) 7 x 8 = 56	(3) 10 x 12 = 120	(4) 3 x 8 = 24
(5) 9 x 6 = 54	(6) 1 x 9 = 9	(7) 24 x 2 = 48	(8) 18 x 3 = 54
(9) 16 x 2 = 32	(10) 2 x 9 = 18		

Multiplication & Division continued...

(11) 16 ÷ 8 = 2
(12) 28 ÷ 7 = 4
(13) 50 ÷ 10 = 5
(14) 36 ÷ 6 = 6

(15) 30 ÷ 15 = 2
(16) 8 ÷ 4 = 2
(17) 49 ÷ 7 = 7
(18) 100 ÷ 50 = 2

(19) 35 ÷ 7 = 5
(20) 81 ÷ 9 = 9

Name_____ Date_____

Improper & Mixed Fractions

Solve each fraction below to its simplest form.

1. $\frac{1}{2} = \frac{1}{2}$

2. $\frac{2}{10} = \frac{2 \div 2}{10 \div 2} = \frac{1}{5}$

3. $1\frac{3}{25} = 1\frac{3}{5}$ $\quad 1\frac{3 \div 5}{25 \div 5} = \frac{1}{5}$

4. $3\frac{25}{50} = 3\frac{1}{2}$ $\quad 3\frac{25 \div 25}{50 \div 25} = \frac{1}{2}$

5. $4\frac{7}{42} = 4\frac{1}{6}$ $\quad 4\frac{7 \div 7}{42 \div 7} = \frac{1}{6}$

---

6. $\frac{15}{30} = \frac{1}{2}$ $\quad \frac{15 \div 15}{30 \div 15} = \frac{1}{2}$

7. $\frac{81}{9} = 9$ $\quad 9\overline{)81}$ ... $\frac{81}{0}$

8. $7\frac{8}{10} = 7\frac{4}{5}$ $\quad 7\frac{8 \div 2}{10 \div 2} = \frac{4}{5}$

9. $6\frac{6}{36} = 6\frac{1}{6}$ $\quad 6\frac{6 \div 6}{36 \div 6} = \frac{1}{6}$

10. $\frac{8}{32} = \frac{1}{4}$ $\quad \frac{8 \div 8}{32 \div 8} = \frac{1}{4}$

Name_____ Date_____

Area & Perimeter

Mathematic Formulas
Area: L x W = A
Length x Width = A
Perimeter: (2 x L) + (2 x H) = P
2(Length) + 2(Height) = P

Area is the total space within a given border

Perimeter is the border of a given area

Find the area in each problem below. Show your work.

(1) A=392
(2) A=40
(3) A=11,682
(4) A=801
(5) A=5,976
(6) A=450

Area & Perimeter continued.......

Find the perimeter of each problem below. Show your work.

(7) P=65
(8) P=147
(9) P=54
(10) P=35
(11) P=210
(12) A=10

1st to 4th Grade Social Studies & Science Key

The Young Scholar's Book Club

Name_____ Date_____

The Gettysburg Address

Materials needed for this lesson:

Book: *The Gettysburg Address* by Kenneth Richards

You can obtain this book by purchasing it from your local bookstore or check it out at your local library.

Directions: Read the book *The Gettysburg Address* by Kenneth Richards and answer the questions below. (TYS Social Studies 1st to 4th, 1 113.3(a)(4), 1 113.3(b)(7)(a), 1 113.3(b)(10)(1f), 2 113.4(a)(4), 3 113.5(a)(4), 4 113.6(a)(4))

1. Write a short definition of the Gettysburg Address? Short Speech by Lincoln on Nov. 19, 1863 to dedicate the national cemetary at Gettysburg.

2. What was the major problem between the Northern States and Southern States during the 1850's? Slavery.

3. In 1860, who was elected president of the United States? Abraham Lincoln

4. Was this president democrat or republican? Republican

166

---

5. What was this president's position on the problem the Northern and Southern States had in 1860? He will not abolish slavery where it already exists. He will not let it spread to new territories.

6. After a president was elected in 1860 what did some do states before he was inaugurated? They left union and started the Confederate States of America.

7. Which states took part in the event? S. Carolina, Lousiana, Texas, Florida, Mississippi, Alabama, Georgia.

8. What was the Civil War and what caused it? A war between the North and South over slavery.

9. When did the Civil War end? The Civil War was from 1861 to 1865.

167

The Young Scholar's Book Club

Name_____ Date_____

What is a Democracy?

Materials needed for this lesson: Any history book or encyclopedia

Directions: Read information about Democracy from an encyclopedia or history book and answer the questions below. (TYS Social Studies 1st to 4th, 1 113.3(a)(4), 1 113.3(b)(1)(a), 1 113.3(b)(11), 2 113.4(a)(4), 3 113.5(a)(4), 4 113.6(a)(4))

Questions:

1. Write a short definition about Democracy? A system of government where people can vote and choose their own representation in government.

2. Who rules in a Democracy? The people, The citizens

168

---

3. Name two other forms of government used in other countries? Monarchy, oligarchy, Republic, Anarchy, Democracy.

4. What form of government does the United States have? Democracy

5. What form of government does Russia and Africa have? Federation.   Democracy or Republic

6. How does democracy work? Majority rules. The people vote for representation in their government. The candidate with the most votes wins.

7. What name is given where no laws or government exists? Anarchy

169

The Young Scholar's Book Club

Name_____ Date_____

United States Government: 3 Branches

What are they? Executive, Legislative, & Judicial

Materials and Books: American Government and Politics Today by Steffen W. Schmidt or any government or history book or encyclopedia.

The United States has a government that operates with three branches. The three branches of government are Executive, Legislative, and Judicial. Each branch has a different function and all depend on each other. The Executive branch involves the president and his roles, the Legislative branch involves congress and their roles, and the Judicial branch involves the Supreme Court and their roles. (TYS Social Studies 1st to 4th, 1 113.3(a)(4), 1 113.3(b)(1)(a), 1 113.3(b)(10)(1b), 2 113.4(a)(4), 3 113.5(a)(4), 4 113.6(a)(4))

The Young Scholar's Workbook Book 1 Vol. 1 www.rysbook.com

Questions:

1. Give 5 roles that the president of the United States has within the Executive branch. Commander in Chief, Make Treaties, Appoint Judges to Supreme Court, Fill vacancies in Senate, Inform Congress on State of Union.

2. The Legislative branch is made up of two bodies. What are they? 1. Senate 2. House of Representatives.

3. Explain the process of how an idea becomes law. Bill introduced to House + Senate. Once Senate and House approve bill it goes to president to sign or veto. If president vetos the bill, Congress can override veto by two thirds majority vote in house and senate.

171

---

4. Explain the roles of Congress. Make laws for nation, Levy Taxes, maintain a military, Coin money, Set standards of weights + measures

5. Explain the roles of the Supreme Court. To interpret or explain laws of Congress and the Constitution.

6. What does impeach mean? To call into question the conduct or integrity of a person.

7. Why would a president be impeached? Conviction of Treason, bribery, or other high crimes and misdemeanors.

172

The Young Scholar's Book Club

Name_____ Date_____

Our Solar System: 9 Planets

Materials and Books: The Big Book of Space Discovery by Schmidt-Cannon International. You can also use any science book or encyclopedia.

Our Solar System is made of 9 planets. These planets are Earth, Mercury, Venus, Mars, Saturn, Jupiter, Pluto, Neptune, and Uranus. Astronomy is the study of the planets and objects beyond the earth. Those who study the planets and stars are called astronomers. They use the telescope to help with their research. (TYS Science 1st to 4th, 1 112.3(a)(4)(5), 2 112.4(a)(4)(5), 3 112.5(b)(11)(c), 4 112.6(a)(5)(6))

Questions:

1. What planet do we live on? Planet Earth

2. Name the smallest planet in the universe. Pluto

174

---

3. Which two planets have a special ring around them? Saturn + Uranus

4. How many days does it take the planet earth to rotate around the sun? How many days does it take Jupiter? 365 days.   12 years

5. Which planet is the furthest from the sun? Which Planet is the closest to the sun? Pluto.   Mercury.

6. Who was the first U.S. astronaut to travel in space? Who was the first woman? Alan Shepard, Jr in 1961 Sally Ride in 1983

7. Who were the first astronauts to land on the moon? What day and year? Neil Armstrong and Edwin "Buzz" Aldrin in 1969.

175

Mercury- Venus — Earth - Mars

Jupiter- Saturn- Uranus- Neptune- Pluto

Name_____ Date_____

Using the Microscope

Materials and Books: You can use any science book or encyclopedia. It is also helpful to have a microscope.

The microscope is an optical instrument having a magnifying lens for inspecting objects that are too small to be seen by the naked eye. (The Random House College Dictionary)
(TYS Science 1st to 4th, 3 112.5(b)(3)(a)(b))

Questions:

1. List 9 parts of the Microscope:

eye piece   Revolving nose piece
Adjusting screws   objectives
Arm   stage
Tube   illuminating mirror
                   Stand

2. Circle the object that can only be seen through a microscope:

a. orange   (b.) bacteria   c. truck   d. butterfly

---

3. What does the prefix *micro* mean?

Small

4. List 5 things that you can only see through a microscope

Viruses, bacteria, organisms, cells and atoms.

5. Write a short paragraph of how to use a microscope.

Answers will vary

Name_____ Date_____

Electricity? Who? When? Where? Why?

Materials & Books: You can use an encyclopedia, dictionary, or any science book.

Have you ever wondered where electricity comes from and why it is an important resource in our society? Electricity is a powerful force in our universe. It has always existed from the beginning of time. It took man to discover and find ways to utilize this mysterious resource. In this activity you will investigate and answer the question that was presented at the beginning of this lesson. Where does electricity come from? You will also do further investigation to find out who discovered electricity and what are some uses for it? (TYS Science 1st to 4th grade, 3 112.3 a(1)(2) b(2)(c) b(2)(b)(d)(b)(c), 3 112.4 a(5) b(2)(b)(f) 3(c), 3 112.5 a(5) b(1)(a) b(1)(c) 4 112.6 a(1)(2) b(2)(a) b(5)(a))

Read the questions carefully and fill in the blanks with the correct answer below.

1.What is the definition of electricity? basic form of energy. Electrical current of protons, neutrons and other charged particles.

2. Who is given credit in history for discovering electricity?

Benjamin Franklin

3. How & why was electricity discovered? rubbing material together to produce electric sparks and properties of attraction and repulsion. Scientists wanted to know what produced the discharge.

---

4. What is a lightening bolt? electricity in action a discharge of an electric charge in a cloud.

5. Who was the first scientist to start experimenting with electricity?

William Gilbert

6. What was the name of the book he wrote to report his findings about electricity?

De Magnete

7. Which century did scientists finally begin to make progress in understanding electricity?

The 18th Century

8. What did scientists store electricity in to contain and study it?

The Leyden Jar

9. Name 3 other ways electricity is contained and stored for use? batteries, electrical generators + charge storing devices in washers, dryers, radios.

10. What do we use electricity for today? To light places at night, appliances, medical machines and transportation.

11. How did people survive in the past without electricity? They used kerosene lamps and wood furnaces.

Scientific Method

Science projects will vary.

Scientific Method

Science projects will vary.

Writing Section

Stories will vary.

About the Author

Brenda Diann Johnson is the CEO/Founder of The Young Scholar's Book Club. The Young Scholar's Book Club is an education organization that offers a free online educational program for Pre-K through 4th grade. The program offers reading enrichment, tutoring assignments, vocabulary building skills, analytical and critical thinking skills and a whole lot more.

The Book Club started with Pre-K through 4th grade in mind. Ms. Johnson's vision is to help elementary students, Pre-K through 4th grade read more, increase their vocabulary, learn how to analyze and critique what they have read and have fun in the process of learning.

Ms. Johnson hopes to give any student around the world who joins "The Young Scholar's Book Club," encouragement, the tools to do better on assignments in school, a broader vocabulary, a love for reading and exploring new information in books.

The Young Scholar's Book Club can be accessed online at www.tysbookclub.com. The curriculum program runs from August to May each year. Students also enjoy summer workshops and seminars.

Ms. Johnson has a B. A. Degree in Broadcast Communications and a Masters of Education Degree in Curriculum, Instruction & Assessment.

194

Ms. Johnson is also the Founder/CEO of ASWIFTT Enterprises, LLC. She is an experienced educator who has taught and tutored Pre-K students through college. Ms. Johnson is the Dean of Education, Curriculum & Instruction at Best Practices Training Institute (B.P.T. I.). She has also authored books and articles.

Ms. Johnson currently lives in Texas with her family.

196

A RISING STAR....

Diamond Starling
Born: 12-25
Hobbies: Reading, Writing, Singing, Swimming, Basketball & Saxophone

Diamond is the daughter of Brenda Johnson, who is the founder of The Young Scholar's Book Club. Diamond has the desire to become a pediatrician. Diamond loves to use her creative writing abilities to write manuscript pieces like her mom. She is an honor student.

She made commendable ratings on her state TAKS tests. Diamond is looking forward to a bright future. She is a smart, intelligent and beautiful young lady. Samples of Diamond's writings radiate a Bright & Rising STAR.

Story by Diamond
My Trip to Austin

My Trip to Austin

By Diamond Starling

Austin is a great place to visit while learning about Texas History. During my visit in 2006, I learned many things.

My first stop was the State Capital Building. The Capital was very old. The paintings located inside of the capital had lots of details and showed our Texas history. Governor Rick Perry works on the first floor in the west wing of the Capital. Governor Perry was not in town on the day of my trip to Austin. Since he was not in town, Royce West was chosen to be governor for the day.

Royce West is actually a state senator. A state senator is someone who holds a state office and represents his district in the state congress. There were many people speaking well of Royce West. They said he is a good lawyer, father and grandfather.

My second stop in the capital was the house chambers. It is the biggest room in the

Capital. It is known as the symbolic heart of the Capital. The governor, senators and representatives debate in the house chambers on different bills waiting to become laws.

Many years ago, the Texas Congress passed the "Don't Mess With Texas" law. I learned the capital is full of interesting information. During my Austin visit, I saw more than two hundred girl and boy scouts. They were visitors at the capital too. I am glad my Girl Scout leader took me to Austin. This was an interesting and exciting trip. I hope you visit Austin someday too!

Educational Books(EBOOKS)

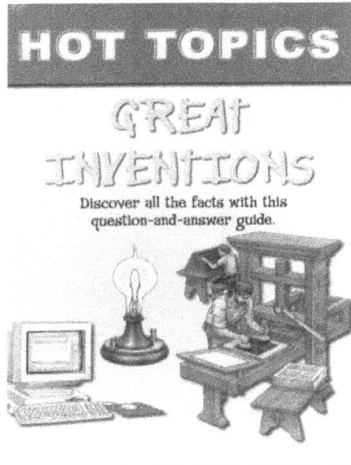

HOT TOPICS

GREAT INVENTIONS

Discover all the facts with this question-and-answer guide.

It is exciting to learn about great inventors and their inventions.

$8.50 plus s/h

GI

HOT TOPICS

PLANET EARTH

Discover all the facts with this question-and-answer guide.

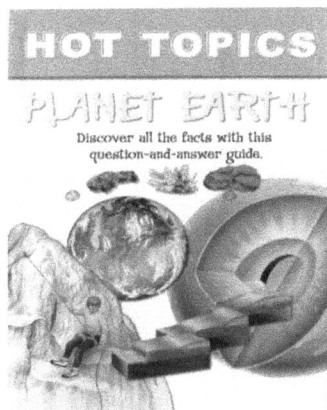

We live on the planet Earth. Learn more interesting facts about the Planet Earth.

$8.50 plus s/h

PE

HOT TOPICS

WILD WEATHER

Discover all the facts with this question-and-answer guide.

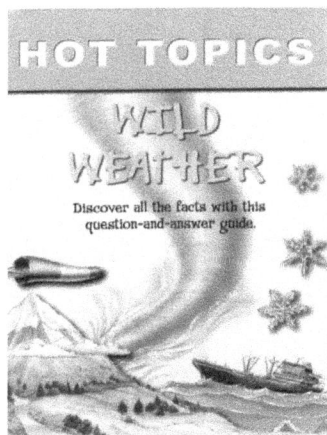

Weather changes daily. Learn more about weather changes in this book.

$8.50 plus s/h

WW

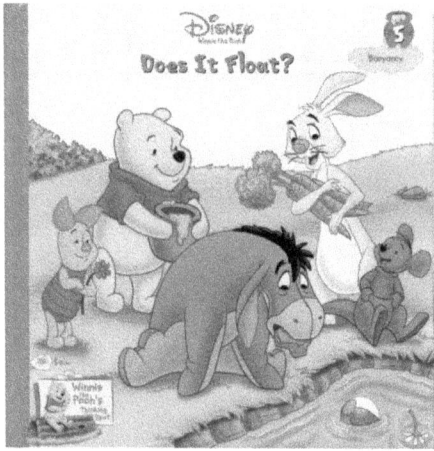

It is exciting to learn why
and how things float.
Your child will have fun
learning what floats.

$6.50 plus s/h

DIF

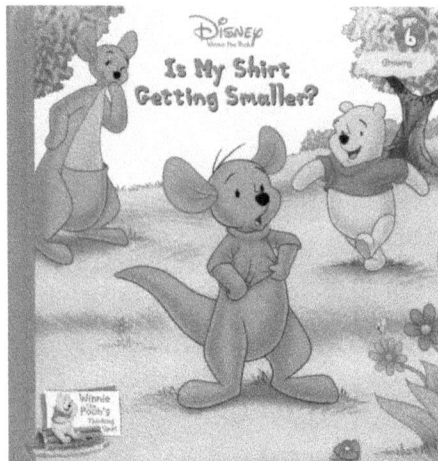

Your child is growing up
and is getting taller. Read
this exciting book on
growth.

$6.50 plus s/h

IMSGS

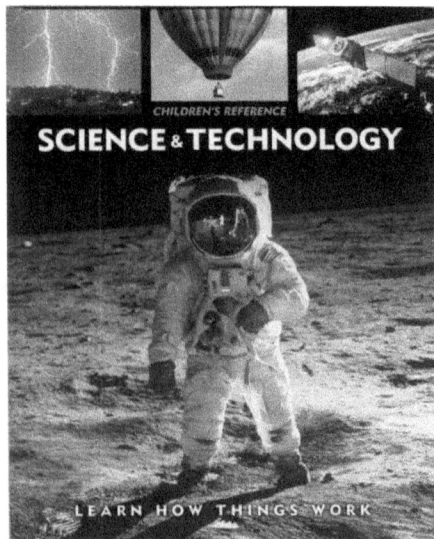

Your child will learn many
things in the core subject of
science and technology.

$9.50 plus s/h

ST

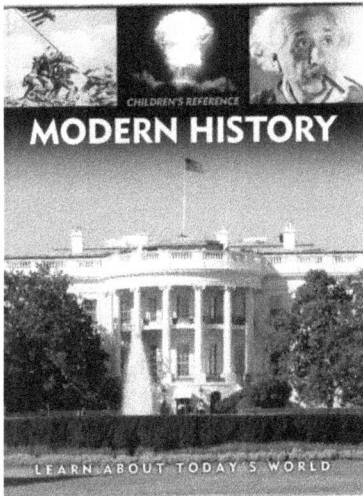

Have hours of fun reading interesting facts in Modern History.

$9.50 plus s/h

MH

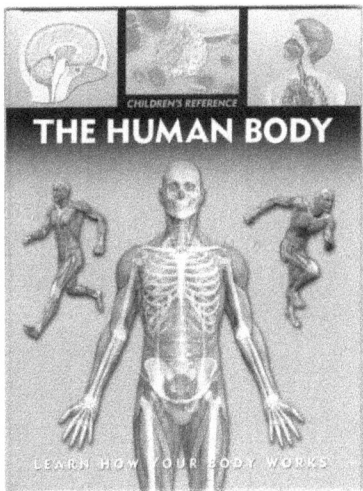

Learn about the anatomy of the human body.

$9.50 plus s/h

THB

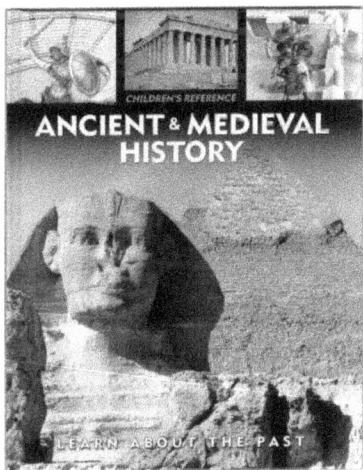

There is much to learn about Ancient and Medieval History.

$9.50 plus s/h

AMH

The Young Scholar's Book Club Order Form

Name_____

Address_____

City_____

State_____

Zip_____

Item Number_____Amount_____

Item Number_____Amount_____

Item Number_____Amount_____

Add Shipping and Handling of $4.00 per item.

Total:_____

Make Checks, Money Orders, Cashier's Checks out to:

The Young Scholar's Book Club
P.O. Box 380669
Duncanville, Texas 75138

Credit Card Orders:

Circle One: Master Card   Visa   American Express   Discover

Credit Card Number_____

Exp. Date_____

Three Digit Security Number on back of Card_____

Name & Address Associated with Credit Card:

_____

Product will ship 2 to 4 weeks once order is processed. Direct concerns on orders to: tysbookclub@yahoo.com Thank you for your business! Make copies of form.

www.ingramcontent.com/pod-product-compliance
Lightning Source LLC
Chambersburg PA
CBHW080501110426
42742CB00017B/2962